INDIAN FLINTS

of

OHIO

Lar Hothem

Hothem House Books
Lancaster, Ohio

Acknowledgement: Many thanks are due my wife, Sue McClurg Hothem, for technical help when the computer and I parted ways. Her assistance was not only welcome, but invaluable.

a 77
.101
Not

Additional copies of this book may be ordered for $11.95 plus $1.00 p. & h. from the publisher at the below address. Ohio residents, please include appropriate sales tax.

Hothem House
PO Box 458
Lancaster, OH 43130

Introduction

From all available evidence, the land area that is now the state of Ohio has had human occupation for at least 15,000 years. It began with the gradual retreat of the great Wisconsin glacial ice sheets, when the Paleo Indians, makers of fluted-base points, came in from the south and southwest. They were followed by the Late Paleo lanceolate-makers, the Plano peoples, who entered from the west and northwest.

Exactly when Paleo (big-game hunting) times ended and Archaic (hunting and gathering) times began is a matter of some controversy. Without reviewing the arguments, the Author is satisfied with an 8000 BC date, which roughly begins the 7000-year Archaic period. This was followed by Woodland (Adena, Cole, Hopewell) and Mississippian (Ft. Ancient, Sandusky, Whittlesey) periods. Finally, about AD 1600, came Contact times, the coming of Europeans and the beginning of historic times.

From the huge numbers of chipped artifacts being found, the region that is now Ohio must have supported large Indian populations. The area had an abundance of the four requirements for life in prehistoric Ohio. These were: Water, for drinking, cooking and transportation; wood for fires, tools and shelter; wild game for food and clothing; flint, for knives, scrapers, drills and points. Of all the surrounding land areas, Ohio undoubtedly had the largest and best deposits of high-grade flints for the Indians to use.

The two major flints are Flintridge (Vanport) and Coshocton (Upper Mercer). Flintridge is famous for its rainbow colors, high translucency and gem-quality swirled material. Coshocton, the well-known "Ohio blue", has a range that includes mottled blues and whites to greys and blacks. Nellie and Warsaw flints are Coshocton varieties, usually in greys, charcoals and blacks, often with banding. Coshocton and Flintridge materials together account for at least half of all prehistoric Ohio Indian flints.

Minor flint sources include: Bisher, dark grey and often banded; Boggs, near-white to grey and black; Brassfield, light-colored and porous; Delaware, mottled tans and browns; Logan, brown specks against cream; Plum Run, tan with reddish inclusions; and Zaleski, brown-black to jet-black. Local river pebbles were also utilized, as well as some crypto-crystalline materials from the glacial deposits.

3

Neighboring states also contributed flints for Ohio's Indians by trade or travel. Counter-clockwise, Michigan had a range of cherts for northwestern Ohio, while Indiana provided Indiana green with pale greenish stripes on a cream ground, and Indiana hornstone in many shades of grey. Kentucky provided Carter Cave flint, in oranges, yellows and ambers that rival Flintridge. West Virginia produced Kanawha flint, semi-dull and black. Pennsylvania contributed glossy chocolate-colored flints, and grey and brown cherts. Even New York state offered Onondaga in blue-veined grey, yellow and speckled.

Now, about *Indian Flints of Ohio.* Most previous books or articles about the state's flint artifacts have been somewhat technical, intended for a limited readership. They often covered a broad field, with limited attention given to Indian flintwork. The author has long felt, after 30-plus years of collecting and study, that a basic, easy-to-understand book with actual photographs of authentic flint specimens has been needed. Therefore, this book is a combination approach, pulling together as many flint artifact types as possible. This has been done from four different major areas of knowledge. These are:

The collectors' commonly known terms for certain pieces are used, and some have been around for many years. Already published descriptive names are employed, these dealing with certain flint traits or periods or both. Official names are used when available, but such names — especially for many Archaic pieces and a few Paleo — are too often obscure, contradictory, confusing, overlapping, or simply do not exist.

Finally, when none of the above sources served to properly identify a flint type, the Author, as a matter of necessity, supplied a description and a name. Such examples are marked with an asterisk (*). In this way, prehistoric Ohio's Indian-chipped artifacts could be covered as completely as possible. A number of flint tools vital to the long-ago lifeway are also included.

All artifacts pictured are from the Author's collection, personally found or carefully acquired over many years. No reproductions or restored flints are shown, and examples may be considered typical for each type. Most are permanently marked on the reverse as to origin so the provenance is not lost. One-inch grids in each photo provide scale, and page-bottom numbers indicate reference publications and appropriate pages.

Some of Ohio's known flint types are not included, simply because good representative examples were not available for

4

photographs. Among these are: Anzick, Buck Creek, Buzzard Roost Creek, Collateral lanceolate, Cumberland (fluted and unfluted), Ross County fluted, Quad, and several others.

However, a very large number of types are here, including nearly fifty that, so far as is known, are named for the first time. This gives the reader a good idea of Indian flints that were made and used in prehistoric Ohio and the ancient eastern Midwest. It should be noted that many, if not most, of the hafted (basal notched, or, stemmed) artifacts appear to be knives, large and small. And many unnotched knife forms show basal indications (configuration, size, thinning) for a handle. Today we have only the blade portions of these knives or points, created in nearly indestructible flint.

While researching the book, the basic goal was not just to photograph and describe most of the known Ohio types of flint artifacts. Neither was it merely to produce the most comprehensive flint artifact listing for any state ever done. Instead, the main goal was to provide a guide for the person who picks up a prehistoric Indian flint and wonders two things. What is it? and When was it made? If *Indian Flints of Ohio* answers these two questions, the work has been well worth the effort.

Lar Hothem
Lancaster, OH
1 Jan 1986

OHIO TIME LINE

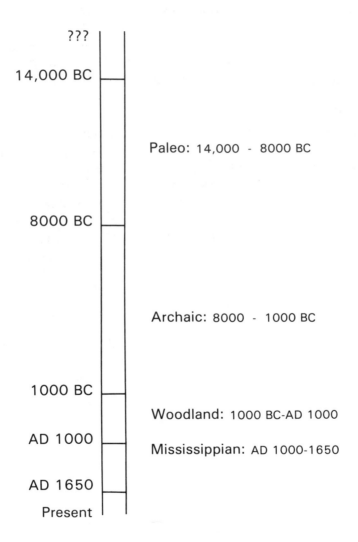

??? |

14,000 BC

Paleo: 14,000 - 8000 BC

8000 BC

Archaic: 8000 - 1000 BC

1000 BC

Woodland: 1000 BC-AD 1000

AD 1000

Mississippian: AD 1000-1650

AD 1650

Present

Note . . . There is a slight overlapping of Time Lines just as there was some cultural carryover from one period to another. To convert BC dates to BP (Before Present, or years before today) add 2000 years. To arrive at AD dates BP, subtract the date from 2000.

CONTENTS

WOODLAND

MISSISSIPPIAN

ALL, AND MIXED PERIODS

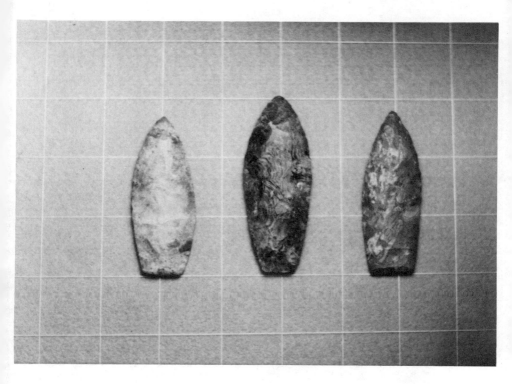

While similar to some other tapered-stem lance forms, the Agate Basin is yet distinctive. It is often shorter, always thicker and with a smaller base. While baselines can be convex or concave, many Ohio examples are straight, as in above examples. There is a dorsal ridge on one or both faces and usually little attempt at basal thinning. Lenticular in cross-section, these pieces have heavy edge-grinding for at least 1/3 total length. Agate Basins in Ohio are both rare and beautifully made. Origin, l. to r.: Morrow, Marion, and Knox Counties.

Ref. 5: pp 48-49. 57: pp 2-3. 65: p 20. 84: pp 141-142.

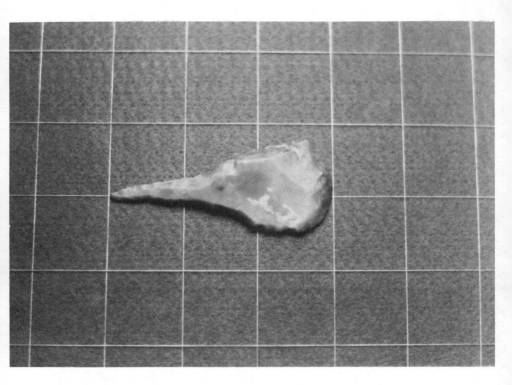

This is perhaps the rarest Combination Tool from Paleo times in Ohio. A possibly related specimen just under 2 in. long from the Vail Site was termed a "unique implement", and, an "awl". It was much thinner than the drill forms found. An awl would also fit nicely with the scraper end, the tool serving both to curry and perforate hides. Another Awl-scraper was found on Virginia's Williamson Site, where it was termed a "borer-scraper". It also was just under 2 in. long, and as with the above piece, the awl was opposite the end-scraper on a long, uniface flake. The example shown is of fine Flintridge, and from Franklin County.

Ref. 21: pp 128-129. 55: pp 23-24.

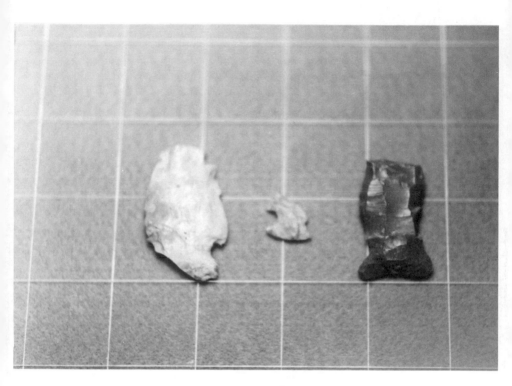

Usually made on badly damaged points or blades, burins provided a very strong and sharp tip. A special indirect-percussion stroke was used, which took off a sliver-like spall, long and narrow. This left a keen edge that was used until it dulled, whereupon another burin was rechipped. Some examples have multiple burins, others only one. Most examples seem to be made on broken tools of known Archaic types, though an occasional little-modified flake will have such a faceting scar. These tools are easy to overlook unless the unique chipping scars are recognized.

Ref. 11: p 8.

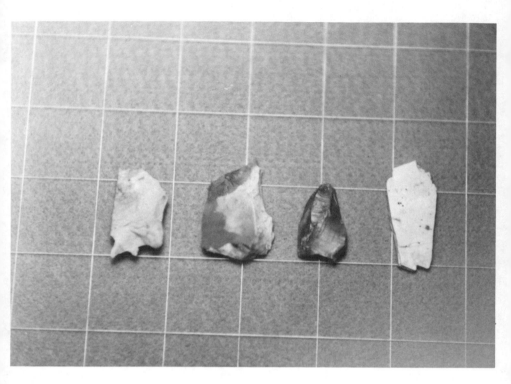

Extremely rare, Burins—Flakes are just that, burins on fairly large flint flake edges. Always on one of the sharply angled corners, the fracture-chipped working tips are the same as appear on broken and salvaged artifacts. One side of the corner is often a snapped edge, smoothed by abrasion. The burin side has the typical short faceting stroke ending in a hinge fracture of small size. Since many flakes received damage and have various flake scars and hard-to-explain fractures and corners, etc., close examination is required to detect these mini-tools.

Ref. 5: pp 80-81. 37: pp 154-155.

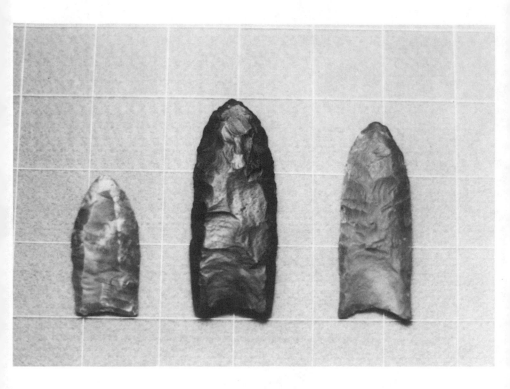

This type almost needs no description, being an Eastern member of the Clovis family. It has been called "Fluted-base" and "Ohio Fluted", and there are a number of Ohio varieties. The base is concave, sides straight to excurvate, and basal grinding is always present. The Ohio Clovis form does not have the elongated ears of some Eastern varieties, but is usually well-made and carefully fluted on one or both lower faces. Some examples have multiple narrow fluting instead of one major flute. No one subtype seems to be exclusive to the state. A wide spread of flints was used, including some out-of-state materials. Photo provenance, l. to r.: Coshocton County, Wayne County, Fairfield County.

Ref. 18: p 19. 58: p 78. 65: p 13.

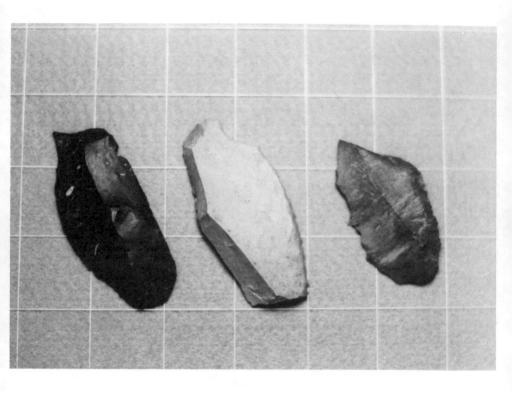

Again constructed on Uniface Blades, these are artifacts that serve two or more functions. Almost always, a knife-edge is included, this in almost any outline, but often excurvate. With this blade edge, the tool may also have semi-circular shaft-scrapers or spokeshaves, end-scrapers or graver tips. A knife-graver was recovered from Hardin County's Mathewson site. In the photo, left, a prize four-in-one example is seen. It combines a straight knife edge, end-scraper, excurvate-edge blade and graver tip. Of fossiliferous black flint, it is from Fairfield County.

Ref. 5: pp 80-83. 36: pp 44-45. 65: p 40.

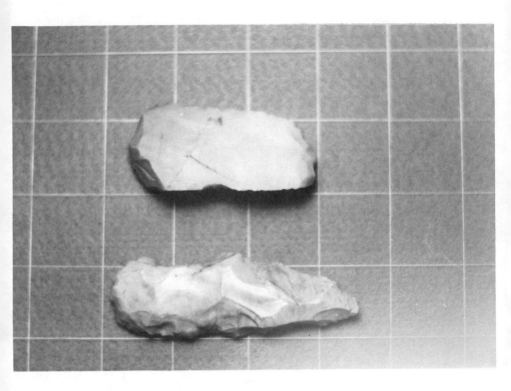

This is a large type that, once its characteristics are known, is easy to identify. It is a long, thick uniface flake with one end (usually the wider) terminating in an end-scraper. Occasionally that portion is spurred. On the uniface body, one or both sides may be chipped into a knife edge, again mainly from the obverse face or top. The smaller end may form a rounded, squared or pointed tip. These are not merely elongated end-scrapers, but always have a major knife edge or true blade. One was found on the McCune Site, Athens County. Another came from the Mathewson Site, Hardin County, and they turn up irregularly elsewhere in Ohio.

Ref. 51: pp 67-68. 65: p 40.

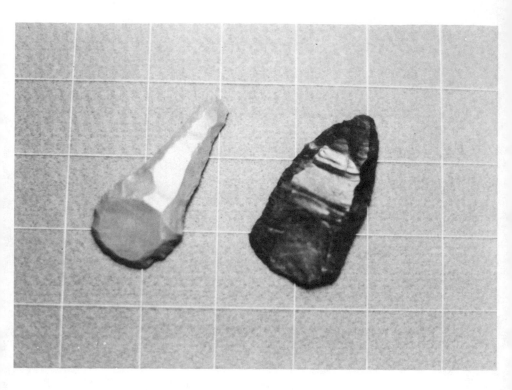

These are large end-scrapers, with a uniface reverse. The obverse is fluted in two places, from two directions. The lower face is fluted in from about the scraper-edge center, while the upper face (shaft) is fluted in from the smaller end. There is a higher, irregular ridge where the two flutes meet. The purpose of the opposing fluting is unknown. These pieces are assigned to the Paleo because of their large size, the fluting, and a certain resemblence to End-scrapers on Blades. There may also be worn-down graver spurs at the scraper corners. These are nearly unique pieces and few are found in Ohio.

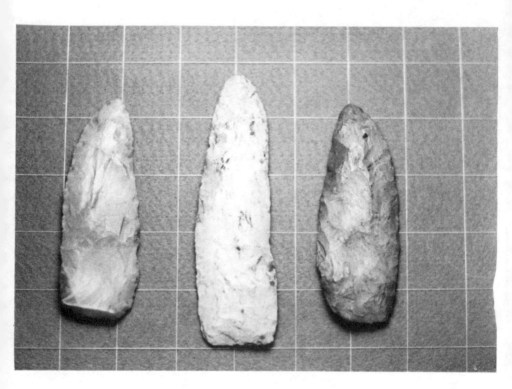

This is a large blade, with one carefully chipped excurvate edge and a backing edge that can have different lines. The straight base can be squared, but often angles more toward one edge. Whatever the size, basal width is about 1-1/4 inches, and light grinding is present. Paleo affiliation is indicated by the unusual flints and cherts used, and random find circumstances. Some examples have basal flutes, and a minor number have an angled, ground-in chipping platform at the base. Angled at an average of 60-degrees, this was for fluting or massive basal thinning. The General Purpose type may be related to the Anzick, which has a straight, squared base.

Ref. 35: pp 12-13. 58: p 18.

Two of three related types from the Hi-Lo Site in Ionia County, Michigan are shown, the Stemmed and the Triangular. All are Lanceolates in outline, with heavy basal thinning instead of fluting. The forms illustrated have the typical concave base. Left and center have small and shallow corner-notches. Chipping is well-executed on most pieces, and there is a wide variety for the type. Basal grinding is present on all examples, and tips are not sharply pointed. The notched form is similar to the Union Side-notched of the Southeast. Ohio Hi-Lo examples are often made of a tan flint.

Ref. 4: p 19. 11: p 15. 58: p 183.

Lance-like in configuration, these Plano Complex pieces are long, fairly narrow and unfluted. Bases on Ohio Examples are often straight, but may be slightly concave. They are generally smaller at the base than maximum width which is about mid-section, but rechipped and salvaged examples can have greatest width nearer the tip. Most are quite thin for size, typically 3 to 5 inches, and thus fragile and prone to breakage. Basal-edge grinding is often present, but is lacking on some. The Honey Run Site in Coshocton County's Walhonding Valley produced many broken specimens, as have other Ohio excavations.

Ref. 61: pp 248, 251. 65: pp 20-21.

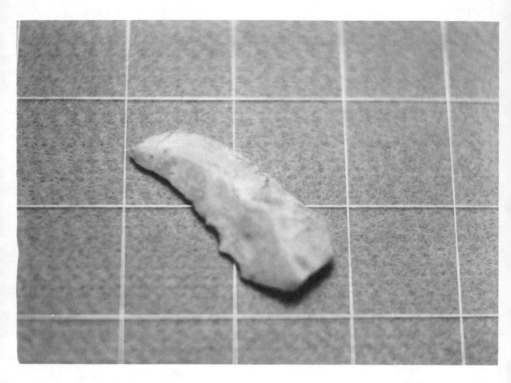

Yet another of the myriad tools from earliest prehistoric Ohio, the Lancet is rarely encountered. It is made on a uniface flake, usually thick and elongated. The base or hafted end may still retain the face of the original core, and the basal region may have dulled edges. The main Lancet feature is a hooked or beak-like working end, very carefully retouched on one or both faces, one or both sides. The incurvate and excurvate edges may have wear, and the above example also has a spokeshave near the base of the incurvate edge. The purpose of these strange objects is unknown, but they have been found over a wide region, from New Mexico to Virginia to Ohio.

Ref. 54: pp 27-31.

McConnell
(Stemmed Lanceolate)

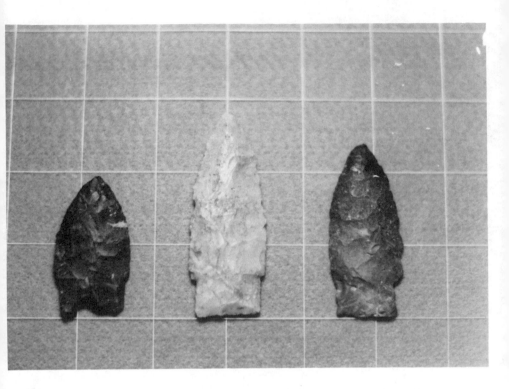

A general type, this artifact greatly resembles the Scottsbluff Type I, which may be of comparable age. The Ohio form is long, narrow and with definite shouldering, the base forming a stem. The stem sides are straight, the base bottoms straight or incurvate, and greatest width is at or near the shoulders. Basal edges are ground. Many of this type are beautifully made, with fine chipping, though a large number are broken when found. On campsites, approximately 5 bases are found for every tip section. The type is sometimes referred to as McConnell Lanceolate, after a Coshocton County site. A range of material was used, some of unknown origin.

Ref. 11: p 12. 51: pp 71-72, 94-95. 58: p 348. 65: p 41. 84: p 133.

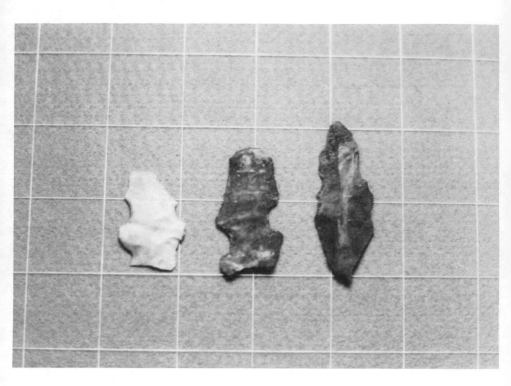

This is another tool type easy to overlook in terms of ancient origin. The shaft-scrapers or spokeshaves are located on an elongated Uniface flake, one or more per side but never exactly opposite so as not to weaken the flake. Spokeshave sides may be steeply chipped or partially created by sheer wear. Six spokeshave examples were found at the Debert Site, each with two concave indentations "staggered" on opposite sides of the flake. Other examples came from the Williamson Site. Some Multiple Spokeshaves are combination tools as well, and also include end-scrapers and/or graver tips. Generally, and with many exceptions, Paleo spokeshaves tend to be larger than Archaic pieces.

Ref. 41: p 102. 55: p 24.

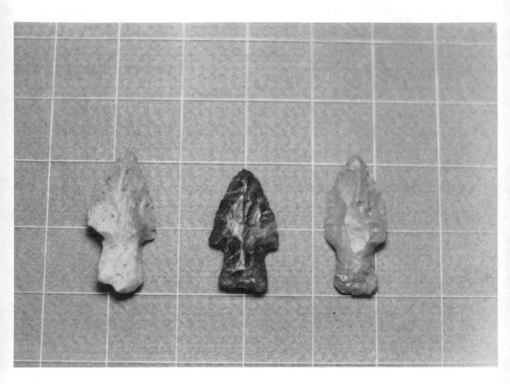

Despite an appearance that does not correlate closely with other Late Paleo artifacts in Ohio, these small points or knives are indeed Paleo. Similar examples associated with Late Paleo artifacts were found at the Stringtown Site, Franklin County. The Keiser Paleo Site in Tuscarawas County produced 25 pieces. These are all short and thick, with a short blade and long, wide stem that often expands toward the base. The stem is about 2/5 the total length, and the base is irregular to fairly straight. The Paleo Long-stem has the stem sides and base heavily ground. Materials are the same as for same-area Lanceolate points.

Ref. 49: pp 12, 13 fig. 3.

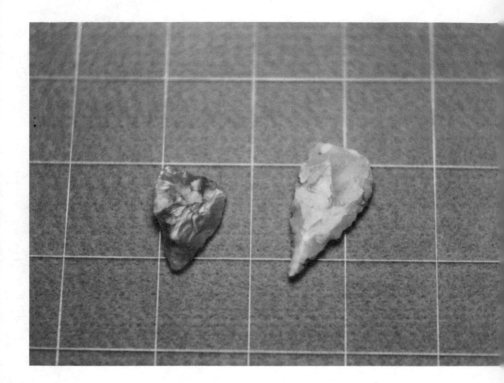

Widely used, the Perforator is yet a distinctive tool. While they are sometimes referred to as drills, there are a number of differences. The working tip is usually much shorter and wider, and lacks the regular and uniform drill taper. Perforator shafts are not three- or four-sided, as are drills, though the extreme tip may be. A number of these artifacts are made on thick flakes, while others are made from portions of broken or exhausted tools. A rare few specimens may be notched or stemmed. These were likely used for holing leather, skins or boring shallow holes in wood or slate.

Ref. 5: p 87.

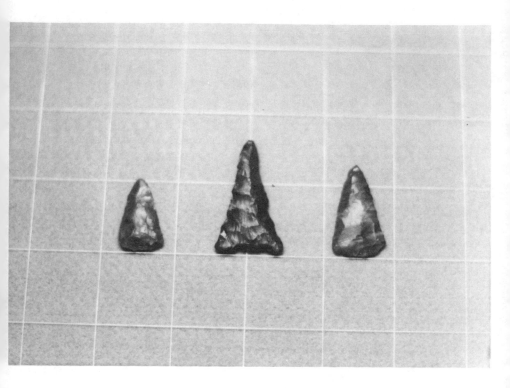

Found in all periods, Salvaged Tips most often began in the Archaic where they are identified by chipping style, thickness and occasional edge-beveling. Tip sections of broken but resharpened knives were picked up by later cultures and the bases reworked to form new points or tools. Some resemble Mississippian triangles but retain the thickness and beveling of their Archaic origin. After reworking (sometimes there is patina disturbance) the basal edge is straight or excurvate. The "new" chipping may be less well done than the earlier work. Fluted points reworked in Archaic times are also known.

Ref. 65: pp 19-20.

These are much like the end-scrapers of later Ohio Indians, except the material corresponds to that used by Paleo groups. In addition to the uniface construction, smaller hafting end with bulb of percussion and larger convex scraping edge, they may also have a small graver spur at either edge corner. (On some examples, when one graver became worn, another was put in on the opposite corner.) Spurred End-scrapers were found at the Lanceolate-producing Honey Run site and at many other Ohio excavations. They have also been reported from the Vail Site, Maine, the Debert Site, Nova Scota, and from elsewhere. Their association has been with fluted and unfluted points alike.

Ref. 18: p 20. 21: pp 134-135. 41: p 186. 64: p 248.

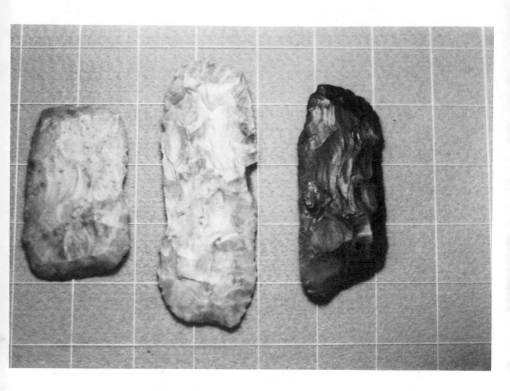

Large, long and thick, these are robust tools from very early times. From 3 to 6 or more inches long and just under 2 in. wide, most are about 1/4 in. thick. Rectangular, the name derives from the squared working end of some specimens, though others are angled or even incurvate. Perhaps the earliest beveled-edge tool in Ohio, the small working surface is sometimes quite sharp. The opposite end, the base, may have hafting indications, such as edge contraction and basal thinning, including fluting. Unusual, even exotic, materials are typical. This form probably continued into Archaic times.

Ref. 11: p 16. 20: pp 32-33.

In addition to the classic type, there are a number of other Ohio stemmed lanceolate forms. All have slightly different basal configurations. Most have stems that expand in width toward the shoulders. While there are perhaps a dozen different variations on this general theme, here are five main types:
1. Straight base.
2. Incurvate base.
3. Straight base, graver spur on base corner (Stringtown type).
4. Straight base, graver spur on both corners (Stringtown type).
5. Straight base, protruding but not spurred corner(s).

This is an extremely large and varied family, and one that would benefit from detailed classification.

Ref. 11: p 13. 18: p 21. 65: p 42. 85: pp 60-61.

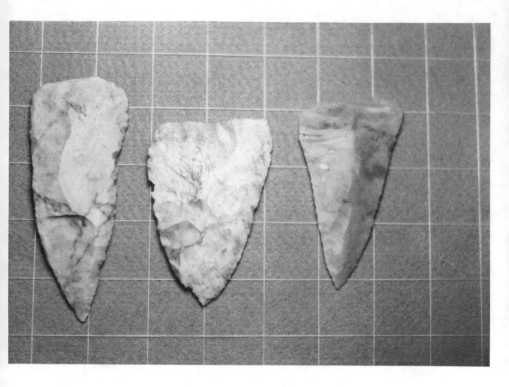

While at least one example was found at the Williamson Site in Virginia and another at the Nuckolls Site, Tennessee, this is also an Ohio type. Due to a unique strike-off technique, the large core-flake is triangular, the reverse slightly concave. The top or obverse may have large flake scars from previous strikes. Both edges are carefully retouched to give a fine cutting use, and the tip is quite pointed. The base may have polish, if not from grinding from use, and shaft-scrapers may located there. There are two sub-types. Variety A has mainly edge retouch only. Variety B (see middle, above) has further percussion work on one or both faces, and is perhaps a refinement of Variety A. Translucent Flintridge blue-grey was often used.

Ref. 28: p 30.

Long flint bladelets struck from special cores, these knives are 1-1/2 to 3 in. long, and rarely found unbroken. They are Tri-faced, three-sided, usually with one wider and two of equal width. Some examples have edges smoothed at one end, as if for handle attachment. On a few examples, one edge has been pressure-flake retouched. The large number of broken examples suggests heavy use. Photo examples were picked up by the Author in Ohio's Walhonding Valley on Late Paleo and Early Archaic sites, and are of Coshocton County materials.

Little is known about this type in Ohio; the name comes from the great similarity to the Clovis-Eastern, except the flute is absent. While it was once thought that poor material prevented fluting or the points were simply too thin to flute, most seem to be made without fluting in mind at all. For some purposes, fluting may have been an unnecessary refinement. Unfluted-Fluted differs from the fluted in two other characteristics. They often lack extensive basal grinding, and some are carelessly made compared with fluted points.

Ref. 18: p 21. 65: pp 38-39. 67: p 36.

These are generally thick blades struck from large cores, almost always much longer than wide. One end has a percussion bulb from the spalling strike. The reverse is flattish but slightly concave, while the top or obverse may have ridges from other strike-offs. Edge retouch is usually present, from a small amount to complete edge treatment. It is usually on the obverse, but often on the reverse as well. These knife forms have any configuration possible, and they are often found on small and scattered hilltop sites. Working edges may be excurvate, fairly straight or incurvate.

Ref. 28: p 28. 65: p 40.

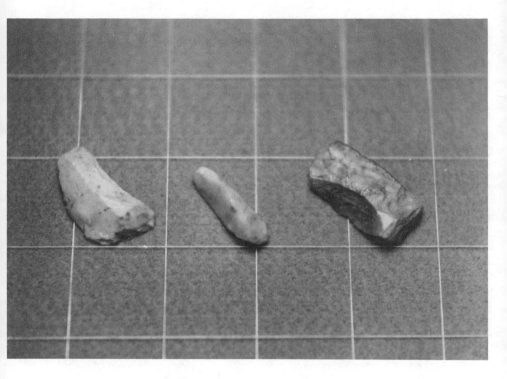

Called "pieces esquillees", these small tools were the third largest tool class at the Vail Site, Maine. They are more scattered in Ohio. Most may have been made from other tools, especially end-scrapers, and many have a concave uniface side from the original scraper. Apparently these were used to split bone and antler, for one end will always evidence battering. The opposite end may be smaller and flat; some wedges were broken in pounding and are quite thin. While "pieces esquillees" wedges are Paleo, several examples have been found on Archaic sites, suggesting a long timespan.

Ref. 21: pp 41, 137.

Chipped flint adzes are sometimes misidentified as crude celts, but they are a specialized woodworking tool from Archaic times. The reverse is fairly flat, while the obverse or topside is rounded or humped. The poll end is generally smaller than the bit end, and the working edge is straight to excurvate. Often this edge is also upcurved due to the rounded shape of the upper face. Most Adzes are roughly chipped by percussion, but the cutting edge — which may evidence battering from heavy use — often has secondary chipping. These pieces are never ground and polished, as were later chipped adzes, celts and chisels of the Ft. Ancient peoples.

Ref. 37: pp 58-60.

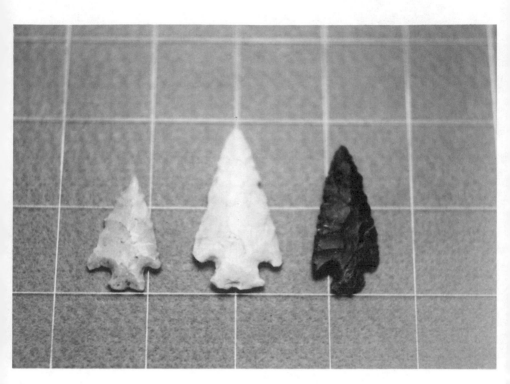

The Amos Corner-notch is long and lenticular, with excurvate to straight sides. The majority are serrated (some pieces have worn-down edges) and sawteeth may be large. Shoulders are very angular to barbed and one may be larger than the other. Notches are large for overall size, and are ground. The base is much narrower than the shoulders and the baseline may be straight to excurvate to irregular. As is the case with other knife forms, the blade may be decidedly canted to left or right. Black, cream and tan flints were often used. The Amos is not a common Ohio type, and may be found lightly intermixed with other early pieces.

Ref. 6: pp 54-55.

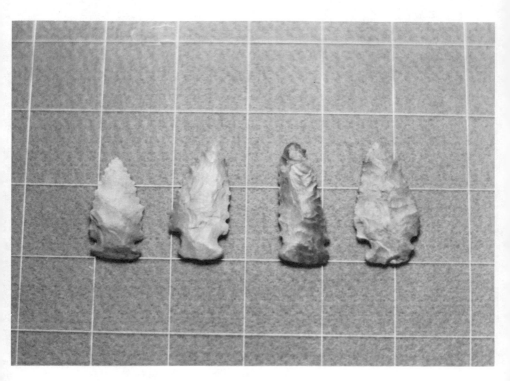

Fairly small, this early knife form is heavily and regularly serrated from tip to shoulders. It tapers from thin at the tip to much thicker at the shoulders, and unsharpened edges are excurvate, the side-notches very low and rounded. Heaviest grinding is in the notches, while the base-bottom is moderately ground. Base corners are rounded. Almost all examples (compared with notching) have blades casually or sharply angled left or right, either a design feature or a resharpening pattern or both. Many Ohio examples are made from light brown or tan flints.

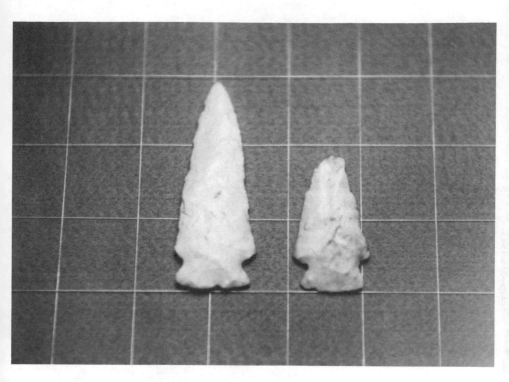

Another of the many Archaic knife forms, this is a long and slender piece with shallow "V"-shaped side notches. Most of the type are very well made, with a straight to slightly excurvate baseline. Basal grinding is present and base corners are sharply angled; at times, these are broken, and give the type a stemmed appearance. Shoulders are not barbed but are angular. Edges are straight or a bit excurvate, depending on the amount of resharpening present. Lenticular in cross section, the type is never serrated. White and cream-colored flints were often used.

Ref. 11: p 24. 76: pp 253-254.

Ashtabula
(Susquehanna)

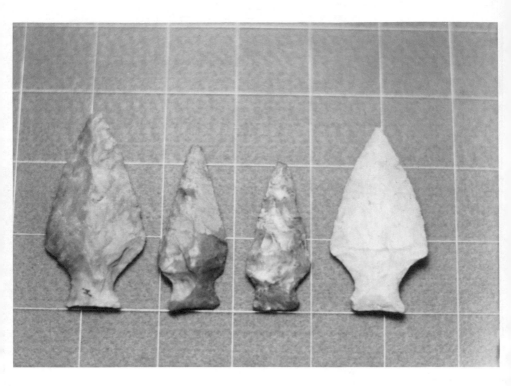

Named for Ashtabula County, this is a northern Ohio artifact that may be found sparcely scattered into central areas. Known also as Susquehanna Broad, it is an Eastern U.S. type. Always widest at the broad shoulders, it has large notches that are somewhat angular. The baseline is straight and the basal region moderately ground. Some examples are lopsided, with blade and tip angled to left or right, indicative of knife use. Chipping is fair to good, but damage to specimens occurs easily at fragile shoulder and base tips. Often quality opaque grey to cream flints were used.

Ref. 5: pp 58-59. 64: pp 140-141. 69: pp 53-54.

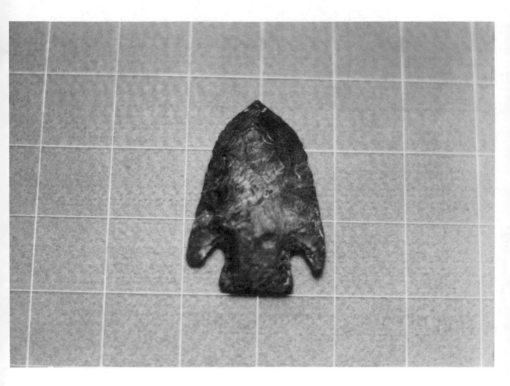

The Classic variety is identified by the large and long notches that form a basal stem. In unsharpened specimens, the shoulders project to the baseline. Heavily resharpened pieces can be identified by the unique stem, which expands slightly toward the bottom. Grinding is usually heavier on the stem sides than stem base. Base-notch Classic examples usually have the abrupt angle reduction of edges near the tip, giving a slight pentagonal appearance. Chipping is invariably excellent and the material of high grades. This Ohio type may be related to other Archaic base-notched knives, such as the Eva.

Ref. 9: p 23.

43

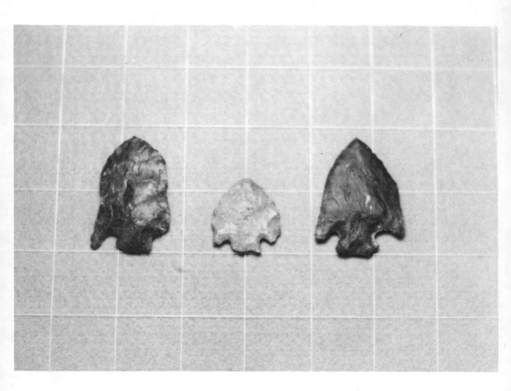

Very little is known about Base-notched artifacts and as a class they are scarce in Ohio. Their main feature is the notching, done on the base bottom. They exist in all sizes and many materials. As with the Classic form, the sides may angle sharply near the tip, giving a blunted appearance. This configuration indicates knife use. The number of types in the General class is unknown, but there are several varieties, including at least one that has fracturing on the stem bottom. For the most part, these are scattered surface finds on Archaic sites and are not found in any concentration anywhere.

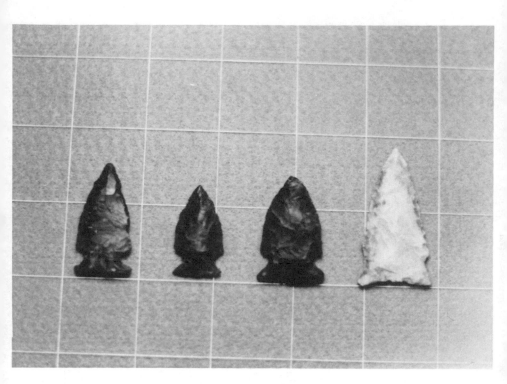

This is the second stage of the Brewerton series of points/knives. The type begins as the Brewerton Corner-notched and is rechipped until the first stage shoulder barbs are removed. Basal corners still project, so it becomes (as here) the Eared-notched. If further resharpened until shoulders are almost gone, it becomes (example, right) the Brewerton Eared-triangular. The other examples are technically Brewerton Side-notched. All have expanded bases and a baseline that is straight or slightly incurvate or excurvate, but the type forms are highly variable. Mainly Ohio black flints were used.

Ref. 50: pp 38, 41. 51: pp 109,111. 64: pp 136-137. 69: p 17.

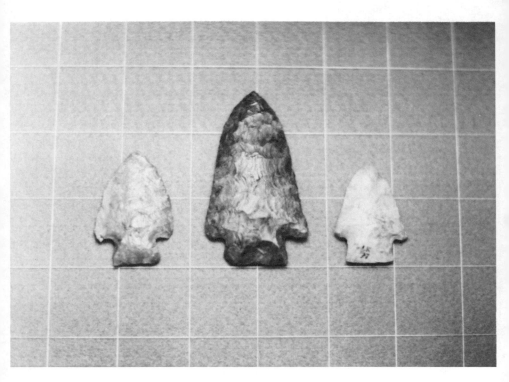

This unusual type has generous corner-notches that form a very wide stem that expands toward the base. Edges are excurvate, shoulders angular or rounded with wear. The tip is often rounded or blunt, typical of knife design. The base is straight and moderately ground, as are the notches. In thickness, the type tapers from thickest just above the notches to very thin at the tip, a form that can be seen from the side edge. Very delicate pressure flaking shaped and finished these pieces, creating very long and shallow face scars. A wide variety of colorful highest-grade cherts was used for the Broad-bladed Stemmed.

Ref. 10: p 23.

Fairly undistinguished, this type yet has a combination of characteristics that establishes recognition. Chief among them is the blade canted or angled to one side. Edges are excurvate on one side, nearly straight on the other. Notches are small and low on the side, and base corners are pointed to rounded. Notches are heavily ground, and the concave to irregular base may or may not be well-ground. Shoulders project slightly but resharpening may nearly remove them. Moderate serrations may be present for the Canted-blade, which is usually well-made from good Ohio flints. The type is occasionally found on small, open Archaic sites.

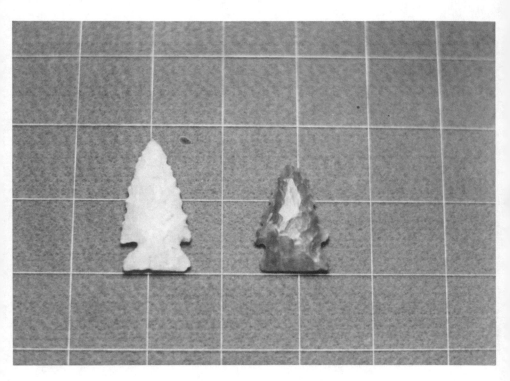

Another of the early corner-notch knives, the Charleston may be related to the Pine Tree which is both longer and later. Edges are straight to recurvate due to the resharpening pattern, are usually serrated, and tips may be rounded. Blades are sometimes off-center. The Charleston is corner-notched but removal of shoulders during resharpening gives some examples a side-notched look. There is a variation in stem widths, but the range is from 1/2 to 3/4 inches. Basal edges are straight to excurvate and are moderately ground. Most Early Archaic flints were used for the Charleston.

Ref. 5: pp 52-53. 6: pp 56-57.

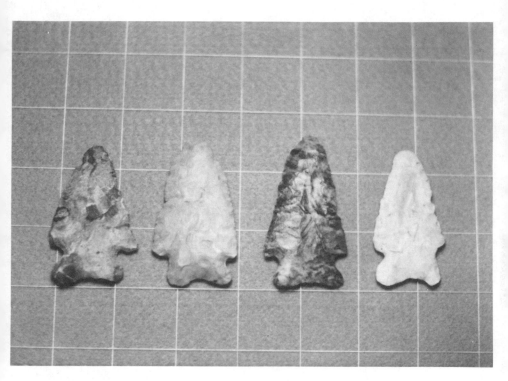

Fairly large, these knives have a greatly incurvate base, rounded basal lobes and a very wide stem. Shoulders may be jutting, but these are reduced as edges were resharpened. The base bottom is moderately ground, notches heavily so. Edges are excurvate but may be straight from rechipping; the two sides can have different outlines on one piece. Serrations are present on some specimens. Several of the type were found at the Indian Knoll Site, Kentucky, which provided three dates in the 4000 BC-2500 BC range. On a few examples, shoulders are removed by fracture-chipping, a hallmark of the Archaic. It is similar to the Early Archaic Rice Lobed of the Ozarks region.

Ref. 11: p 29. 58: p 322. 76: p 253.

This type resembles certain other forms from the same very early period, being thin and rugged. Serrations are always present but may be worn down. Edges are excurvate to incurvate, shoulders barbed and base corners pointed. Corner notches are wide and not always deep. The base is straight to slightly incurvate, often somewhat uneven despite moderate basal grinding. Whatever the piece size, the stem width is between 3/4 and 1 in. across. Basal thinning is present and may be extensive. Tan and grey flints are common for the type in Ohio.

Ref. 11: p 22.

Very little is known about Crescent (or semi-lunate) knives in Ohio. Most have a fairly straight edge and a semicircular top or backing that has edge grinding. This indicates a probable haft in that area of wood or bone, possibly similar to the Eskimo Ulu. The longest proportion is end-to-end, widest at the middle, and thickest at or near the central blade area. There are Crescent varieties, as designated here. Variety A (shortest, above) has a heavily beveled edge. Variety B (largest) has an edge resharpened equally from each face. Minute use-scars indicate that this largest piece was sometimes used in a chopping manner. Crescent knives are from Archaic sites and are scarce finds in Ohio.

The Decatur or Fractured-base knife is distinguished by the basal treatment, and fracturing may exist in four places. When first made, edges are excurvate and resharpening may produce beveling or serrations. Shoulders range from rounded to pointed, and all pieces are corner-notched. The base-bottom is fractured in from each corner, the scars often terminating where several flakes were removed at each side near the center. In addition, one or both notch areas may have fracture-chipping from the outside of the base corners. All this work was perhaps a shortcut to edge-dulling, as basal edges are usually well-ground. There is a large size and blade-shape range for the Decatur in Ohio.

Ref. 3: pp 28-29. 34: p 9. 58: p 101. 80: pp 23-25.

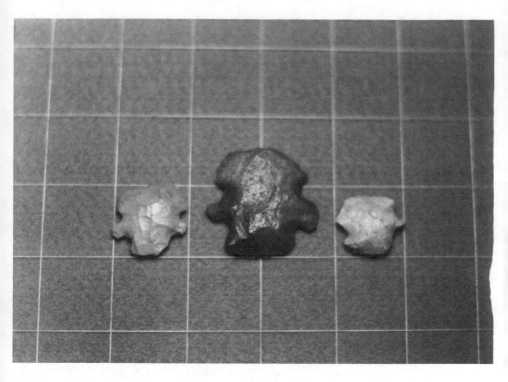

Rather than a whole-made original artifact type, the Double-notch may be a salvage form. The basal treatment is identical to that of the Pentagonal knife, and overall it is a Pentagonal made into a Hafted Scraper, this scraper having additional notches. Apparently, the base was left unchanged and the two side notches put in for extra-secure fastening to the handle. And, except for extra notching, the pieces are simply Pentagonal family scrapers; these sub-types will be found in the same regions. The type is uncommon. The examples shown are made of orange-pink and red flints.

Four Drawshaves were found at Kentucky's Indian Knoll site, and were so-named by a likeness to the carpenter's blade. All were damaged or broken, suggesting heavy use, probably wood-working. While the examples recovered were made from salvaged knives, it was thought that each end might once have been hafted. The working edge shows great care in forming, and resharpening signs may be present. In addition, this tool form may have wear-polish on the working edge. The illustrated example has this feature, plus sharp beveling. Originally it was a large Archaic corner-notch blade. In whatever condition, Drawshaves are not frequent Ohio finds and few sites have produced examples.

Ref. 76: pp 262-265.

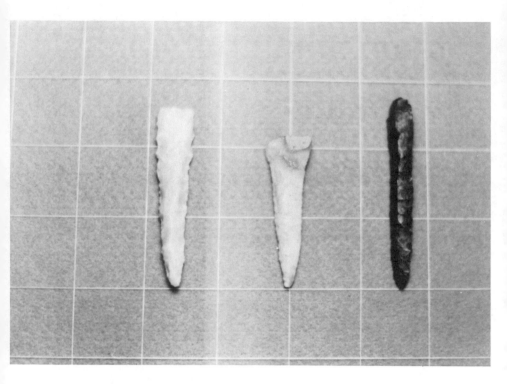

Pin-shaped or cylindrical or straight-shaft drills are known from the Archaic through Ft. Ancient times in Ohio. The simplest drill form, some are of nearly equal diameter at the two ends, while others have a slight flaring and/or thinning at the haft end. Some are sharply pointed, while the working end on others may be dulled. At times, these drills show very little use-polish on the sides as would be expected from their supposed use in drilling holes in hard materials. Shorter Pin-shaped drills may actually be clothing toggles or gorge hooks for fishing, and Ft. Ancient Indians had a double-tipped drill, one at each end. Longer Pin drills may have been hairpins.

Ref. 12: p 184. 29: p 133. 30: p 38. 47: p 432 fig. 2. 76: pp 256-258.

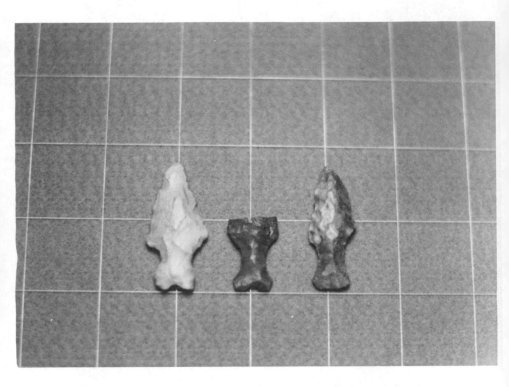

One of a number of stemmed Archaic types, the Elongated-stem has a relatively thin basal stem about ½ in. long whatever the piece size. Edges are probably excurvate, resharpened to straight. Tips, similar to some other knives, may be heavily worn or blunt, and shoulders are angular to rounded. The base of the expanded stem identifies the type, it being either notched or heavily thinned. Base corners may be fracture-chipped off or heavily worn, and this portion is narrower than the shoulders. The stem is usually well-ground. The Elongated-stem is a sporadic find on Archaic sites, and some dark Ohio flints were used.

   Despite the small size and unimpressive form, these are yet
highly specialized tools. Most are less than an inch long, and
made from a broken or snapped flake. The basic triangular form
is enhanced by chipping on thin edges and by abrasion-
smoothing on longer flat edges. Both combine to create a small,
piercing tip, with rapidly expanding sides. This portion of the
End-flake Awls may show heavy use-polish. It is probable that
these tiny artifacts were hafted for maximum efficiency. Examples shown were found on Archaic sites in central Ohio, and
many different flints were used.

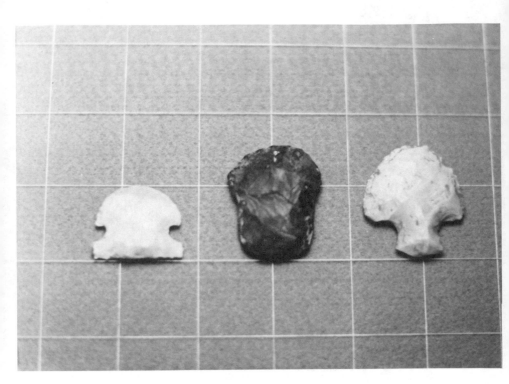

These knives should not be confused with Hafted Scrapers which they somewhat resemble. The rounded working edge is chipped from each face, creating a new edge midway between the faces. (The type is not unifacially chipped, which produces a beveled edge.) The working edge does not typically show scraper-like wear and is usually knife-sharp. A very few examples have serrated excurvate edges. It is difficult to tell if these were purpose-made or are a type salvaged from broken artifacts. A variety of Ohio flints were used for this tool form.

Ref. 70: pp 18-19.

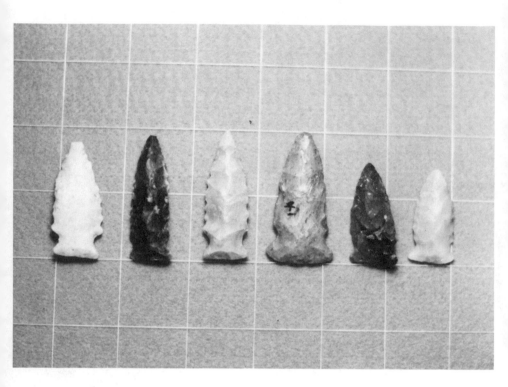

Similar to the Hellgramite of Pennsylvania and the Helton of Illinois' Koster Site, Horizon VI, the Fish-spear is long, narrow and quite thick. Serrations are often present, usually the sign of knife use. Notches are very low and shallow and heavily ground, and the baseline is straight. This is one of the easiest-to-identify Ohio types, as the facial outline is fish-like. A Fish-spear subtype is shorter, wider and thinner, lacking the median ridge often seen on the main type. The subtype resembles the Matanzas to some degree. For both pieces, a very wide range of flint was used, and of the photo examples, each is made of a different material.

Ref. 17: pp 10-11. 33: pp 8-9. 64: p 324. 79: pp 16-17.

These small artifacts are one of the many Ohio mini-tools that usually go unrecognized. There are two varieties. One has a straight edge (chisel), and one has a scooped edge (gouge). Both working edges are formed at the end of a long, narrow flake, with sides snapped off. The haft end may have some edge-smoothing, and the opposite, working edge has been further shaped by abrasion. These are keenly ground at an angle to provide a sharp, beveled cutting edge. These fractional flakes are thicker and stronger than Hopewell Bladelets, and earlier, though the tool type may have lasted some time. Examples shown were found on Archaic sites in central Ohio.

Like most other bifurcates, the Fox Valley has strong indications of knife use. There are four keys to identification. It is extremely thin and well-made, the shoulder tips are often enlarged or upswept at corners, and the base is quite small and rounded. And, the base bottom may have only a tiny indentation, or none. The Fox Valley is less angular than the Lake Erie and lacks basal/shoulder fracturing. It is also thinner and better made than most other bifurcates such as the Kanawha. Found mainly in western parts of the state, the Fox Valley is perhaps Ohio's hardest-to-find bifurcate. White and cream flints are common.

Ref. 4: p 88. 58: p 136. 73: p 204.

This type is long and narrow, and has excurvate edges that are often resharpened to straight. It is ovoid in cross-section and edge-serrations may be present. There are small corner-notches and stems are wide and short. Part of the shortness is caused by fracture-chipping the stem base. While seemingly impossible, this was done in a semicircular fashion, from one or both sides, faceting the entire basal edge and lower base sides. While the Fractured-stem and Decatur both have a similar basal treatment, they do not otherwise have much in common. The Fractured-stem may be early in the Archaic, and related to several Tennessee Valley types.

Ref. 73: pp 134-135, 216. 74.

Named for a now-destroyed Muskingum River site, the Gilbert is a small type that is found mainly in eastern Ohio. Edges are ex-curvate, the baseline straight to convex. There are two varieties, A having shallow side-notches that appear to be well-ground. Variety B is more nearly stemmed, with a wide base. While some are well-made, others evidence a certain lack of care or skill in the making. Found on river terrace sites, they have not been associated with pottery; the type may have a fairly limited distribution. Material for the Gilbert is always colorful Flintridge, often in glossy shades of pink and white.

Ref. 50: pp 16-19.

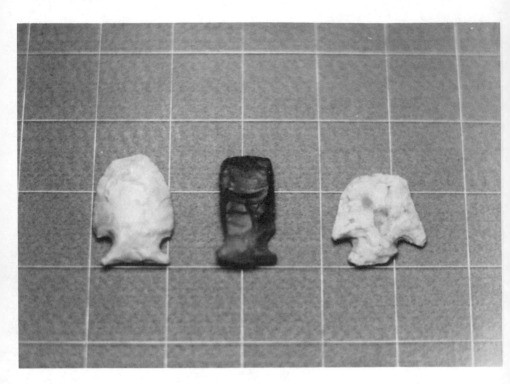

Though these resemble Hafted Scrapers, they differ in several important ways. The (probable) wood-working edge is fairly small, located closer to the former tip than the present base. Unifacially chipped, the edges are not as steeply beveled as scrapers, but are angled at about 30 degrees to give a sharper edge. And the obverse working edge may have additional thinning flakes to give an even sharper edge. There may be use-polish on the lower tool portions near the edge, which is excurvate in relation to the beveling. Hafted Chisels are not uncommon, but often go unrecognized.

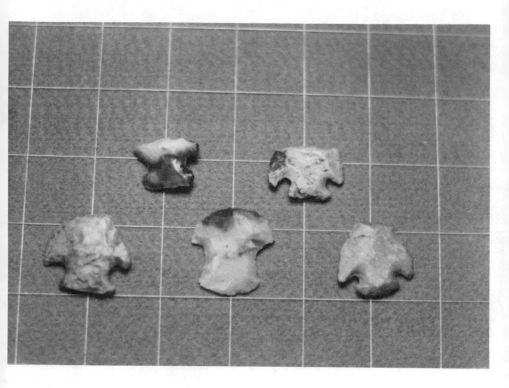

So-called because of the hafting basal notches, this scraper form seems to be a salvaged artifact. While some specimens may have been made as-is, most were likely rechipped from a broken knife or point. Corner-and side-notched pieces are most common. The working edge is unifacially chipped, usually excurvate to some degree, and steeply beveled. The balance of these pieces was left intact. Basal configuration often provides the original artifact type. Hafted Scrapers are most commonly found on Archaic sites; 104 came from the Raisch-Smith surface-collection.

Ref. 47: p 432.

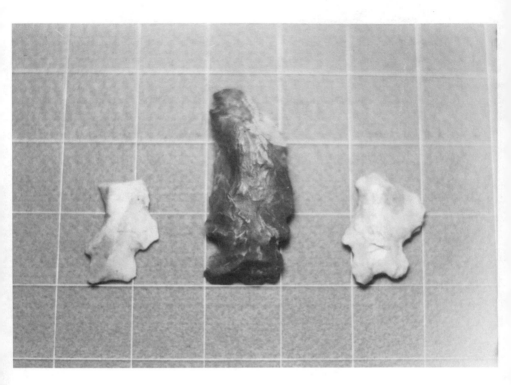

Made from a large curved flake, these tools have an incurvate reverse and an upper face heavily worked. The basal area is side-notched, fairly straight or bifurcated, and is heavily ground. Diagnostic is the large incurvate bevel-chipped working edge, done on the left side so the piece could be reversed and chipped or resharpened from the right. Characteristic of most Shaft-scrapers is a smaller chipped or polished area somewhere on the back portion that was evidently used for finer shaping work. These may be considered Variety A. A Variety B has been described, being bifacial and made from a broken knife or tool.

Ref. 24: pp 165-167. 68: p 113.

The Hardaway Side-notch is a very rare Ohio type, and only a few examples were made here or drifted in from the South where it is more common. Lightly-resharpened edges remain excurvate, shoulders are jutting, and notches are small and rounded. The base is very wide and (like the Recurve-base) the baseline is recurved, concave in the center and convex at the ends. Basal areas are thinned and usually heavily ground, as are the notches. Many Hardaways have a very short, straight-edged blade (see example, Knox County) and are probably exhausted knives. Unknown flints are the rule, and the type is always a chance surface find.

Ref. 56: p 11. 58: p 168.

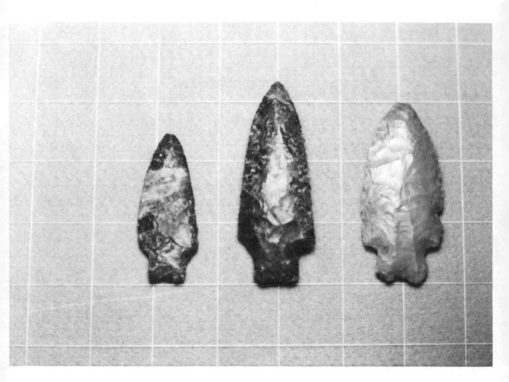

This term has been in use by collectors for many years because of the fairly large and sturdy design of the piece. A medium-size artifact, it has excurvate edges and a broad stem with base bottom that is straight or incurvate. Stem sides are heavily ground, the base moderately ground. True to the name, it is thick, with greatest mass near the rounded shoulders. Basal thinning is present, and long flakes may extend part way up the lower face. Despite thickness, these are superbly made pieces with much delicate pressure retouch on edges. It is very similar to the Eastern U.S. Genesee which may have wider shoulders and a more tapered stem.

Ref. 11: p 47. 58: p 148. 69: pp 24-25.

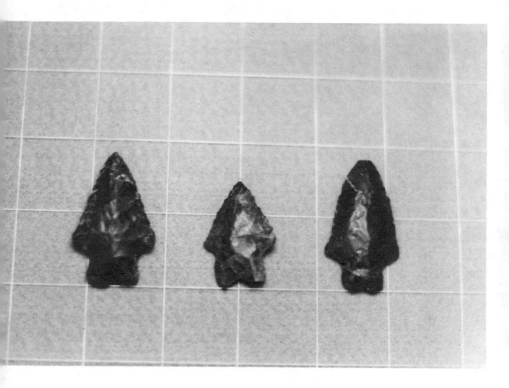

Medium-size, these are thick in cross-section with a sturdy stem that may expand slightly toward the base, the bottom which may be slightly indented. The type is somewhat similar to the Kirk Stemmed-St. Albans found at St. Albans, hence the extreme age. However, the Heavy-duty Serrated of Ohio may have smaller, more regular serrations, may be thicker in cross-section, and overall, smaller. Resemblences of this type to the Heavy-duty (see elsewhere) may simply be fortuitous, since the two are separated in time by the entire Middle Archaic. Dark flints are the most likely material for the Ohio area.

Ref. 6: pp 66-67. 11: p 20. 25: p 23. 58: p 148.

This blade type may be related to the Weak-stem due to the very short base, but appears to be a distinct type. Often a knife form, some blades are thick from biface resharpening, or the blade may be strongly angled to left or right. Corner notches are small, and the incurvate baseline produces basal tips that resemble the shoulder tips. The basal area in contrast to many other Archaic pieces is only lightly ground. Basal thinning is present for the width of the wide stem. Cream and light tan cherts have been used for the type.

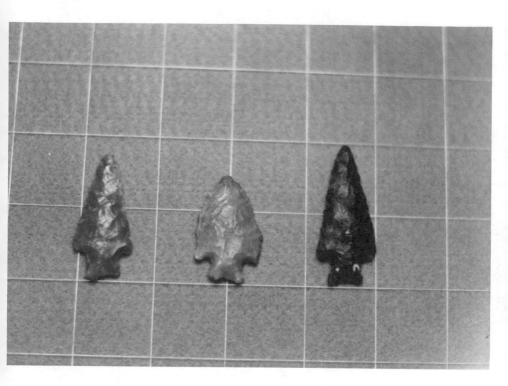

This piece has such large corner-notches a stem is formed
which expands at the base. Widest at the shoulders, unused
specimens have somewhat barbed shoulder tips, though
resharpening rounds or reduces them. Notches and base bottoms are moderately ground and the stem often shows signs of
basal thinning. The base bottom is sharply incurvate, but not to
the degree of most bifurcations. Edge-serration is often present,
and edges are excurvate or straight (resharpened). The balanced
mix of fine percussion and pressure flaking suggests an Archaic
placement.

The Kanawha Stemmed can be distinguished from other Early Archaic bifurcates by greater thickness, short heavy stem, and the unground base. Blade edges are straight to incurvate depending on the degree of resharpening, and shouldering is at 90-degrees or greater. Some shoulders are removed by fracturing, the sign of knife use, and this may be done on only one shoulder. The stem has rounded lobes and bifurcation (Broyles reported 82% with this feature) ranges from slight to moderate in depth. The Stanly may have descended from this type. While most Early Archaic flints were used, the Kanawha is not a frequent Ohio find.

Ref. 6: pp 58-59. 27: pp 229-230. 58: p 197. 60: pp 36, 41.

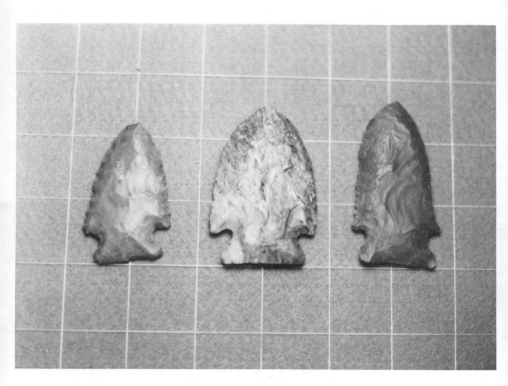

In time, the Type A (Large) is placed after the Charleston and before the LeCroy. It is generally a good-sized blade, with shoulders wider than the base (before resharpening), and both the base and notches are ground. The baseline averages about straight and basal corners are angular to rounded. Blade edges may be deeply serrated, the saw-teeth becoming smaller toward the tip. Some examples have the serrations worn off and a few do not appear to be serrated at all. Some blades may be canted to left or right and there may be unequal edge-wear. Dark flints predominate in Ohio. Note: Types A and B, here, are the Author's designations.

Ref. 6: pp 64-65. 25: p 22. 30: p 28.

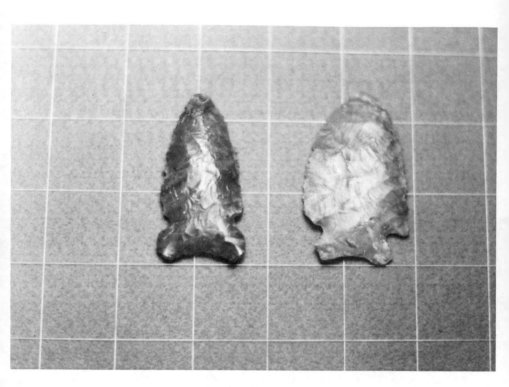

Type B (Large) is somewhat similar to the Kirk Corner-notch Type A (Large) in size, serrations and large, ground notches. Type B, however, has quite a concave base which may be as wide or wider than the shoulders after much resharpening, and the baseline is not heavily ground. Type B made up 77% of the discoveries in Zone 16 at the St. Albans Site in West Virginia. The main distinction is the concave, less-ground baseline. Dispite the high percentage of St. Albans finds compared with Type A, this seems to be a minority piece in Ohio. Unusual materials have been noted, including semi-translucent flints in caramels and greens.

Ref. 6: pp 64-65.

This is related to the Kirk Corner-notch (Large) except in size and base bottom, and is a widely variable form. Edges are serrated, often uniformly, and are excurvate or straight (resharpened). In unsharpened specimens the stem width is about half the total blade length. Notches are wide to narrow, well-done, and the base bottom is straight to excurvate, not incurvate as on some Large examples. Basal area and notches are moderately ground, and most shoulders are sharply barbed. Eastern Ohio dark flints were often used.

Ref. 6: pp 62-63

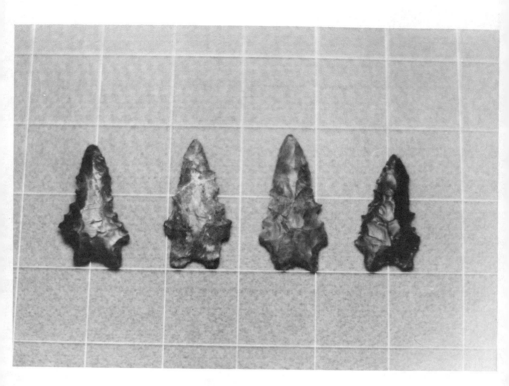

This Kirk Stemmed (named by Coe) is very different from the average Kirk Stemmed pieces from St. Albans; the two are almost separate types, here delineated by variety. The Kirk Stemmed--Coe is of a more uniform size. It has a deeply indented, if not bifurcated base, large, staggered serrations, and a blade that is considerably narrower toward the tip. In this region the serrations may be worn off. Also, one or both bifurcate lobe ends may be fracture-chipped at a sharp angle across the corners. It is found scattered thinly about the state.

Ref. 6: pp 66-67. 15.

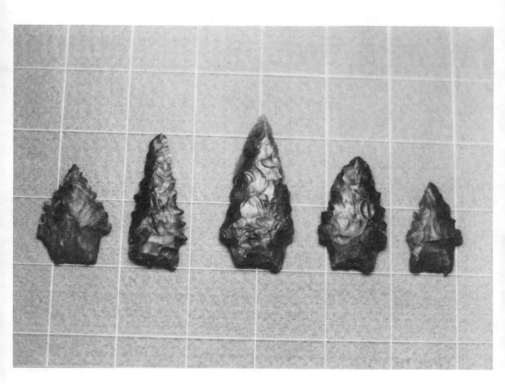

Another very old type, this has a triangular blade and a sturdy base which may be straight or indented but not bifurcated. Stem sides may be straight or expand toward the base, or, the shoulders. The angular shoulder tips of this knife form may be resharpened off, and a few examples are rechipped in as far as the stem; many examples have heavy knife use indications. Some are much shorter than when first made and have a stubby appearance. Serrations are present, sometimes large at the base becoming smaller toward the tip. Dark Ohio flints were commonly used for the Kirk Stemmed--St. Albans.

Ref. 6: pp 66-67. 56: p 17. 58: p 207.

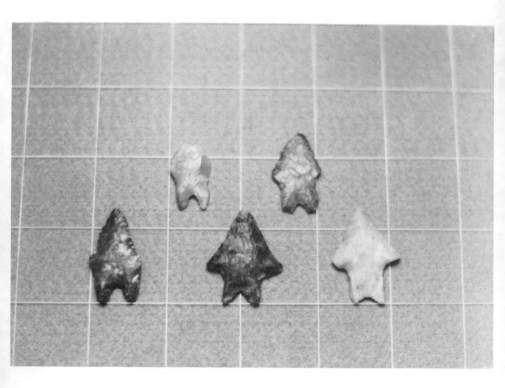

   Generally of small size, this unusual artifact has a proportionately large twin-lobed base and tabular or flat faces. Often serrated-edged, the Lake Erie may be fracture- or sliver-chipped in one or more of four different places. These are, in order of decreasing frequency: At the shoulder tips, on bifurcation outside, on bifurcation inside, and across the base bottoms. An average example might evidence several such areas, and in any possible combination. Knife use signs include blunted tips, angled blades and shoulder-tip removal to maintain edge-use efficiency. Most known high-grade Ohio flints were used.

Ref. 34: pp 8-9. 82: pp 20-21.

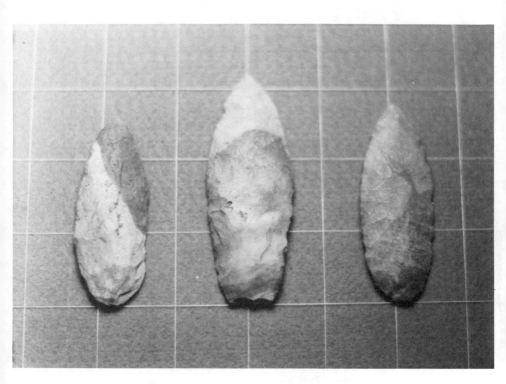

A companion artifact and found intermixed on the same sites with Late Archaic Stemmed pieces, the Lanceolate type greatly resembles some Paleo forms. Many examples appear to be simply unstemmed versions, while others are larger and may be a knife form. All taper toward the base, with widest portion about midsection, and the base is squared or rounded. While resembling the much earlier Agate Basin, there are three differences to avoid confusion. Materials may be unusual and lower-grade, while the average workstyle is inferior. Also, lower edges and bases are not heavily ground, as is common with Paleo pieces.

Ref. 14: pp 22-23.

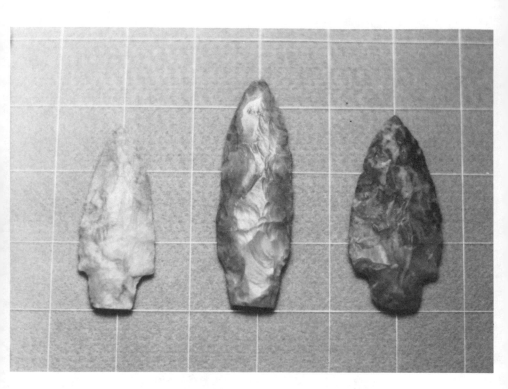

Despite the fairly large size, these stemmed pieces are well made. Examples not heavily resharpened have strong shouldering, but resharpening mades them more narrow. Besides the expert chipping, the type has a sturdy stem that tapers to the base. Stem sides are moderately ground. A distinguishing feature of many is the base, which appears to have been snapped off at an angle, toward one face, giving an angled but flat base. There is no effort at basal thinning the stem, which is nearly as thick as the rest of the piece. Unusual, possibly out-of-state flints were often used.

Ref. 14: pp 22-23.

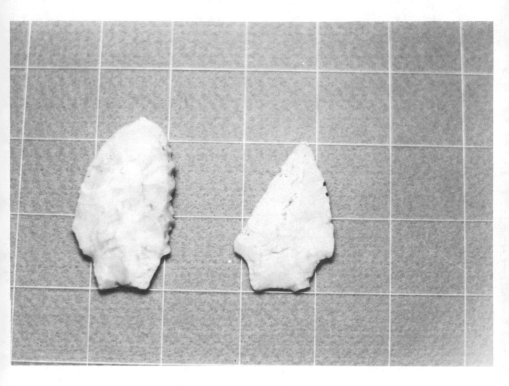

This large knife type has a very wide blade, is fairly thick and may be serrated. Different wear and use patterns can often be seen on the two working edges, which may be a factor in making some tips off-center. Similar to the Tapered-stem type (see elsewhere) the stem is short and contracts toward the base which is mildly bifurcated. Unless the shoulder-tips have been damaged or fracture-chipped off, the piece is widest at this portion. This is still another of the very many Early Archaic blade types that are rugged and multi-purpose.

Ref. 26: p 25.

This early bifurcate type can be recognized by the small size, flat faces and generally unground base. Most are an inch or a bit more in length, though unsharpened specimens are twice that. Quite thin, the blade edges on smaller pieces are resharpened to form a right angle at the tip. Shoulders are usually at right angles, though tips were often fractured-off as the blade became shorter. The base is flat and wide and may constitute half the length on well-used examples. Basal indentation is "V"-shaped and the basal lobe bottoms may be irregular. Darker flints common to the Early Archaic were often used.

Ref. 3: p 64. 6: pp 68-69. 16: p 1.

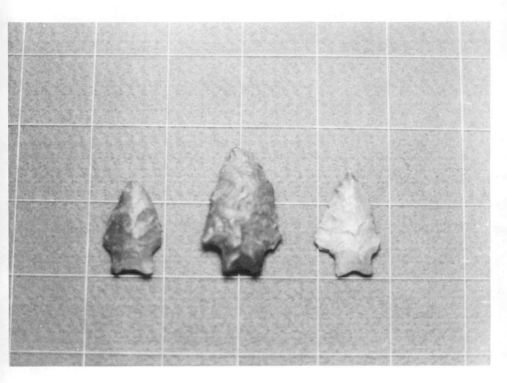

This small knife form has in common a stemmed base with a hint of twin basal lobes or bifurcation. Stem sides are ground, as is the indented base which is the main clue to their extreme probable age. Generally rather thin, shoulders may be wide on some pieces, reduced by resharpening, or removed by fracture-chipping. Many have extensive edge damage, and stem thinning is frequent. While some Lunate-stemmed pieces appear carelessly made, all evidence expert chipping. Whatever their age in the Archaic, the small sizes suggest a specialized knife use. Tan flints are common for the type.

This bifurcate type is almost always serrated, with large sawteeth that may be very worn down. It is extremely wide at the base, with lobe outsides that project nearly as far as the shoulders. This gives a stem between notches that often averages an inch across; the whole impression is of much mass in the basal region. Another early type, the MacCorkle may be positioned between the older Kirk Corner-notched and the later St. Albans Side-notched. Dark Ohio flints plus some cherts were often used.

Ref. 5: pp 52-53. 6: pp 70-71.

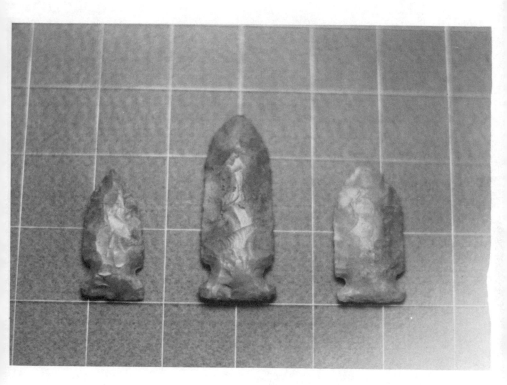

The type has long, parallel straight sides before converging at the tip. The Matanzas is often resharpened from the tip, producing shorter specimens. It is thick in cross-section, randomly percussion-chipped with fine retouch. The base is straight and well-ground, basal corners rounded, and with low-set side-notches. The notches are heavily ground, rounded, and medium-deep. The Matanzas appears in several related forms. In Ohio, tan and brown flints of high quality were often used.

Ref. 58: p 245.

A Late Archaic piece, this may occasionally be associated with Glacial Kame Indians. This knife form is generally large, with excurvate edges (until resharpened) that are often carefully retouched. The side-notching is extremely low, "U"-shaped, and not large compared to overall size. Basal edge is straight to slightly incurvate and moderately ground; notches are heavily ground. The edge is resharpened from both sides, so beveling is not present. Dark tan, brown and grey flints were used, occasionally Flintridge.

Ref. 69: pp 35-36. 72: p 40.

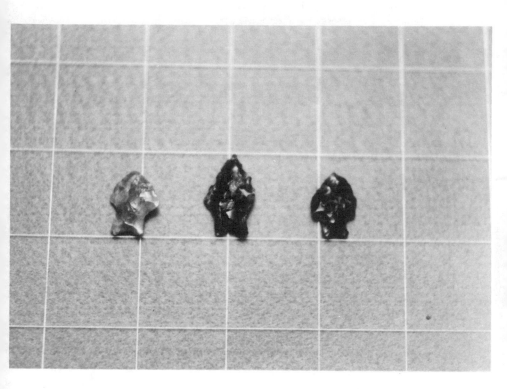

Unlike any other of the many Ohio bifurcate knives, the miniature designation refers to the size of bifurcation, and sometimes, the whole piece. Whatever the artifact size, the base stem is about ¼ in. long and wide. Resharpened specimens are much smaller and relatively thick, and are the most common form, being from ½ to 1 in. long. Incorrectly called Birdpoints at times, this diminutive form is much older than true birdpoints. Basal grinding exists in varying degrees and serration may be present. Bifurcate lobe corners may be fracture-chipped off. Dark flints are common for Mini-bifurcates.

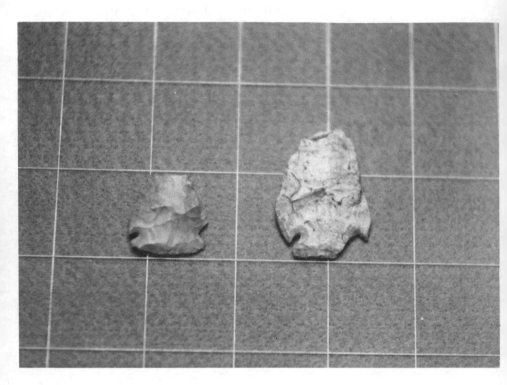

This may be related to an unnamed Early Archaic Illinois type, also with rounded basal corners. It is somewhat similar to the Kessel of West Virginia, which has a concave base and is 7900 BC. The Narrow-notch is very rare in Ohio, the reason two incomplete pieces are shown. Small and thin, the lightly ground base is straight to excurvate. It has two unusual features. One is the notching, 1/8 in. deep and 1/16 in. wide. Another is the shoulder fracture-chipping, which is done up along the outside of the shoulder, along the lower blade edges. This is the only known type to have this unique fracturing. Unidentifiable grey and brown flints were often used.

Ref. 6: pp 60-61. 58: pp 58, 204.

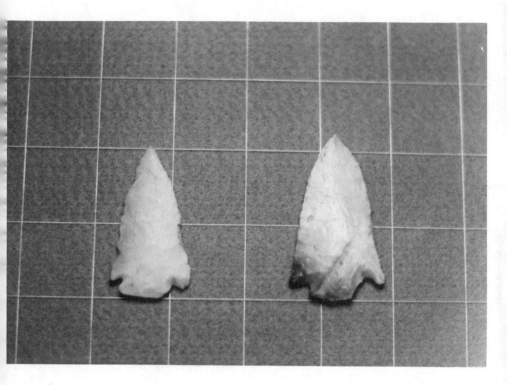

While some examples have been identified as the Unfractured-fractured base and the Franklin County, this piece has some similarities to the Decatur. However, it usually lacks the base-bottom fracture-chipping, has no broad shoulder-tips, and fewer ranges in size and type varieties. It is thin and well-chipped, with a very pointed tip. Edges are excurvate until resharpening, which may be heavy on the lower edges, and serrations may be present. Corner-notching is small and delicate, and shoulders are angular to barbed. The baseline is incurvate, straight or excurvate and moderate grinding is present, as is basal thinning. Ohio may be in the eastern fringe of distribution for the Neuberger.

Ref. 58: p 269.

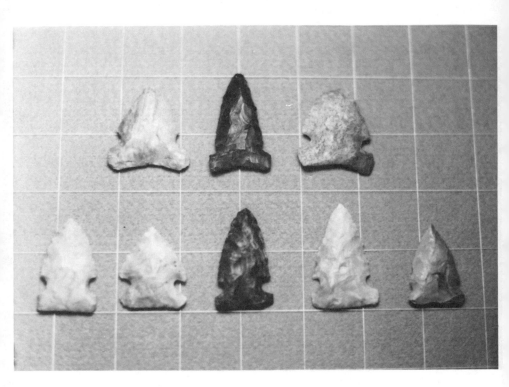

This piece has two varieties, with merging types. Variety A has a fairly straight base, while Variety B has an incurvate base. Otherwise, the two are similar, with a wide, sturdy ground-edge base, ground notches and a fairly short blade. Some examples are nearly as wide at the base as they are long, often the result of resharpening which was usually done from both faces. In unused condition, shoulders match the base in width. Base ends are generally squared but may be rounded or angular. All Ohio flints were used, but Flintridge is unusual.

Ref. 11: p 18. 32: p 10. 58: p 271. 60: pp 37, 41.

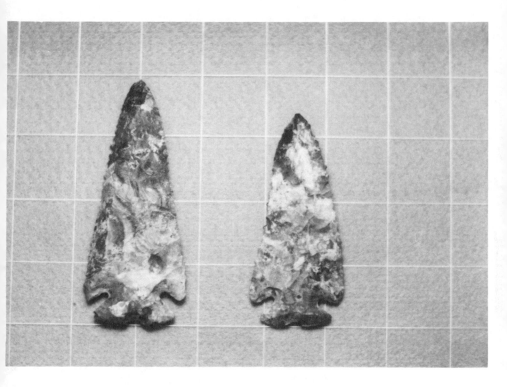

Known also as the Notched-base Dovetail and possibly related to the St. Charles, this yet has a unique form. "Dovetail" applied here is confusing, especially since there is indeed a rare St. Charles sub-type with a notched base. Semantics aside, the Notched-base differs from most Ohio "Doves" in basal configuration, notching and edge treatment. This knife when resharpened is usually both beveled and serrated, beautifully designed and chipped. Notches and base are heavily ground, and the least-well-done feature is often the mid-base notch. This is sometimes chipped mainly from one face. Mottled Coshocton County blue is typical, followed by grey and black flints from the same source.

Ref. 11: p 38.

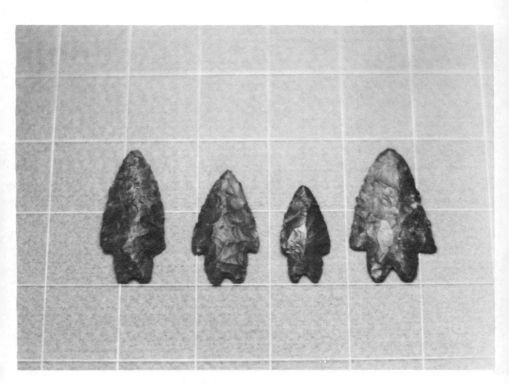

Possibly a variety of a known bifurcate type, the Notched-stem yet has distinctive features. It is usually nicely balanced in configuration, with matching basal lobes and matched protruding shoulders. Shoulder tips are generally not fracture-chipped off for resharpening, and chipping is invariably excellent. Edges are usually finely serrated. Characteristic is the slight notching at the upper stem sides, which may be angled in or up. This sometimes gives the shoulders a pronounced and unusual barbed appearance. Much Upper Mercer from Coshocton County, especially ''Ohio Blue'', was used.

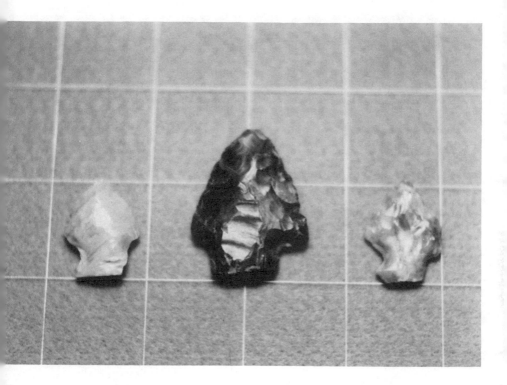

While these may at first appear to be crudely stemmed pieces with little diagnostic value, close examination provides some clues. The origin is a broken blade tip, usually Archaic, with break area still visible on the stem bottom. The large notches appear to be haphazardly placed, in from the corners, and no stem grinding is present. The balance of these pieces is unmodified, sometimes retaining Archaic beveled-edges. Patina disturbance at some notch areas indicates occasional notching in much later prehistoric times. Artifacts with signs of two time periods are most unusual.

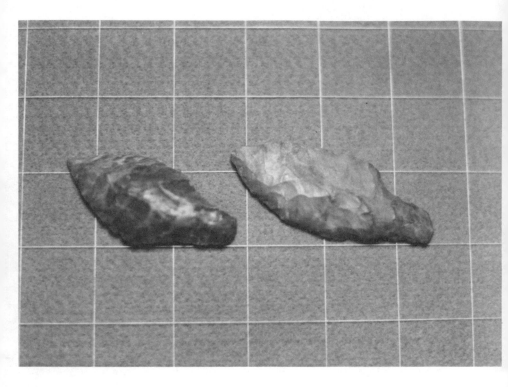

These unusual knife forms were made from large, thick, elongated flakes. The reverse is fairly flat and curved from the original core from which struck. The obverse has a high ridge and most of the percussion shaping was done on this face. The pieces taper to a long stem that angles or is offset to one side. Stem sides have light edge-grinding, and the stem base is rounded. Despite the rather casual appearance, some examples evidence heavy if not long-term wear. This is yet another of many little-known Archaic knife forms.

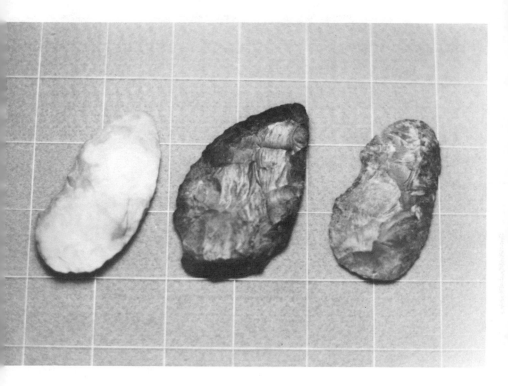

This type is egg-shaped, with a large rounded base and smaller rounded tip. It had excurvate edges and is usually more than half as wide as long. Chipping ranges from mediocre to fine, and one long edge may show resharpening. The base may be lightly ground. Some Ovoid Knives have a purpose-made indentation on one edge, probably made as a shaft-scraper. The type is always well-made and with use-signs, and should not be mistaken for a later period preform. Examples found came from sites that had no slate or stone artifacts, and so may be early in the Archaic.

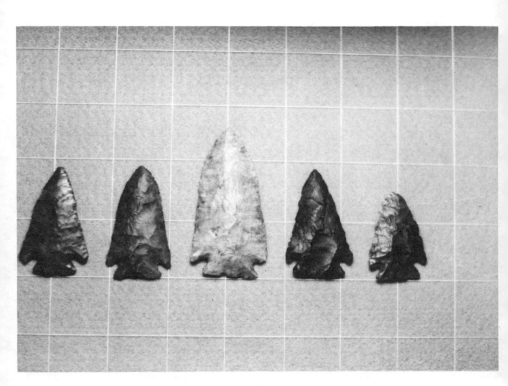

Greatly resembling the much later (2500 BC) Vosburg which has a longer stem and wider notches, the Palmer also is an extremely well-made type. The tapered corner notches are uniform, the base straight or a bit convex, the shoulders barbed, sometimes sharply so. Palmers are often serrated, but these may be so worn as to be indiscernible. Most of the type have an extremely triangular outline, with fairly straight sides. Base bottoms and notches are generally heavily ground, another type trait. Brown, grey and black flints predominate.

Ref. 56: p 12. 58: p 286.

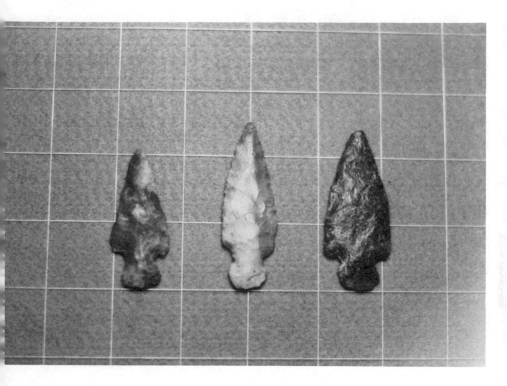

The only Ohio flint artifact with this unusual basal shape, the Pendant-stem has various Archaic features. Edges are excurvate to straight, and shoulders are angular to rounded. A long, narrow type, the base is smaller than shoulder width and equal to blade width about 3/4 in. from the tip. Side-notches are rounded, and the stem terminates in an enlarged and rounded pendant-like form. The notch area is heavily ground, and the stem edges are moderately dulled. Found on a few Archaic sites, little is known about this distinctive type. For the Pendant-stem, brown, tan and black mottled flints predominate.

This is a relatively thick-based corner-notched knife. "Five-sided", the sides include the base, two lower edges and two upper edges that converge at the tip. There is often an abrupt angle change where the two side edges meet, and sometimes a spur. Upper edges appear most-used, and some Pentagonals are resharpened back nearly to the notches. Basal grinding is present, the baseline straight to incurvate, but no major efforts were made to thin the base. Some Pentagonals lack the two blades per side and have the normal one. The Ohio form is sometimes misnamed the Afton, which is a larger Western piece more stemmed than notched. Many grades of drab flint or chert were used, plus some Flintridge striped.

Ref. 58: p. 4. 83: pp 16-17.

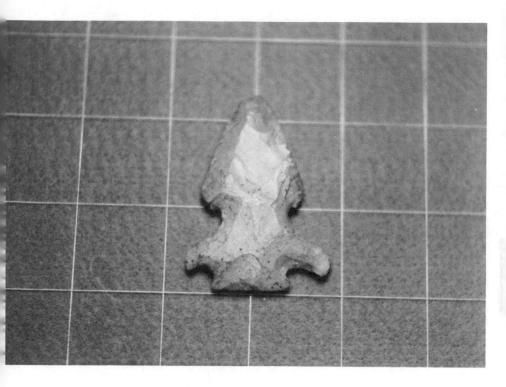

The Pincer-base may be the strangest and scarcest Archaic form in Ohio. There are two varieties, Author's designation. Both have side-notching, usually upswept, and most have an excurvate edge, beveled by resharpening. Both have base corners that curve outward and downward like the jaws of a pincer, and this feature may be exaggerated on some pieces. All basal areas are ground to some extent. Variety A (not shown) has the pincer baseline only. Variety B (illustrated, Pickaway County) also has a protuding central stem, and is the rarer of the two. The Pincer-base does not seem to be a salvaged form, and some are made of unusual flints and cherts.

Ref. 52: p 22 photo.

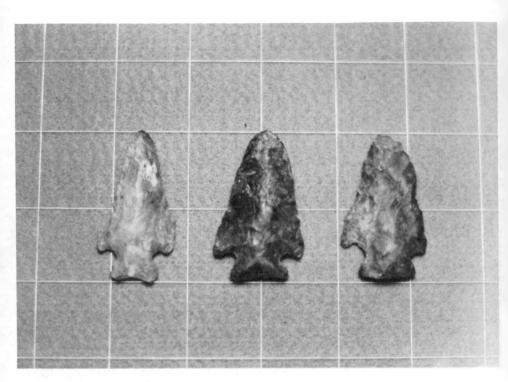

These small knives are similar in many ways to other Archaic corner-notched pieces, but have two identifying characteristics. They have long, angled shoulders, deep and wide notching, and a baseline that typically has a central ridge. The reverse is flat or a plane, and slightly convex. In resharpening, lower portions of the blade were often left intact, giving the edges a two-level profile. For the Plane-faced type, Upper Mercer light blue Ohio flints were often used.

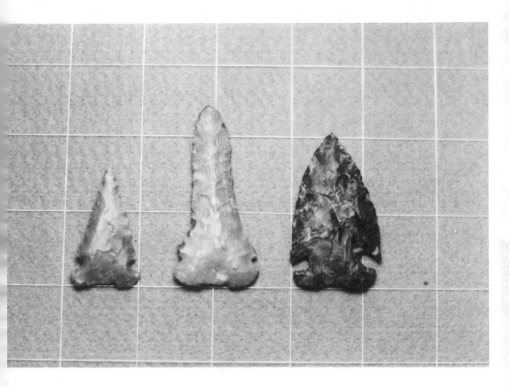

Little is known about this early form. The basal edge, corners and lower notches are well-ground, but the distinguishing feature is the base bottom, which is recurved. It is indented for about 1/2 inch, not notched but with a raised baseline, itself not heavily ground. At this portion basal thinning took place which may extend up into the lower face. If these are a variety of the Hardaway Side-notch, they are 7500 BC-6500 BC. The exhausted blade (on left) resembles a Dalton form from Kentucky.

Ref. 15. 58: p 168.

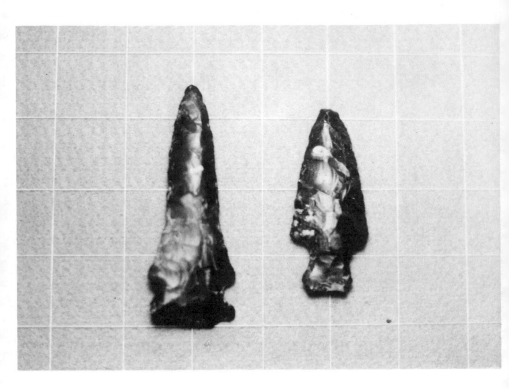

One key to Renotched Pieces is that some resemble no known Ohio type, which is not surprising in that basal features are partially redundant. That is, the base (see photo) retains portions of the original notching. When blades broke at or near the notching, the base was discarded. Then, similar notching was put in at an economical distance above the original notching, which thus salvaged the form for further use. Two keys to identification: The presence of partial notching at the base lower corners, and, basal flatness. What was once mid-blade thickness is usually drastically reduced by extensive basal thinning, but traces of the break area often remain.

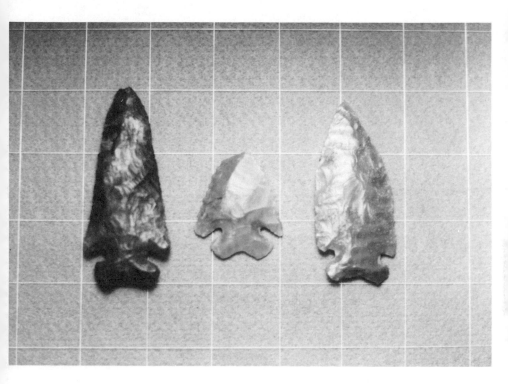

A large blade with excurvate or straight beveled edges, not-ches are deep and low on the sides. Shoulders are barbed and basal grinding is present. Base lobes are rounded or angular and never project beyond the shoulders, being restricted to about 3/8 in. beyond the stem column. This form is remarkably similar (except for the less-wide base) to the Taylor of South Carolina, a type which seems to have a limited distribution there. If related, the Restricted-base dates in the 7000 BC-6000 BC range, Early Archaic. Coshocton flints and some Flintridge were often used.

Ref. 58: p 374.

These are large knives with excurvate to straight edges and a wide base. Width, configuration and basal thinning indicate a handle that did not interfere with edging, which is resharpened to the basal corners. The key to Reverse-bevels is the edge, which begins at the tip as typical right-hand beveling. About mid-length or nearer the base, the edge briefly becomes straight before reversing, or switching to a left-hand bevel. Seen from the edge, this reversal is dramatic. There are at least two types. Type A has a concave base, while Type B has an angled base. Except for Crescent knives, Reverse-bevels may be the scarcest of Ohio's unhafted Archaic pieces.

Ref. 32: p 11.

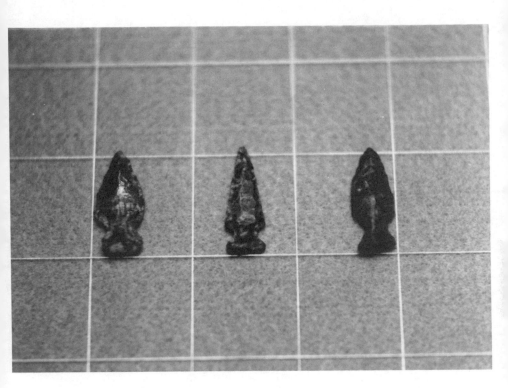

Found most frequently in southern Ohio, the Riverton is a small, thick side-notched point with a variable form. Averaging just over 1-1/4 in. long, sides are excurvate to straight, the base the same. Notching is not large (but appears so because of the small point size) and is always low. Shoulders may be angular or rounded, but never barbed. The base is the same width as the shoulders or less, and basal areas are unground. Some blades and tips are asymmetrical, and some specimens are rough-chipped and/or not well-finished. This type is more common to southern Indiana and Illinois; local materials were most often used.

Ref. 58: p 325. 71: pp 20-24.

These at first glance are very similar to several Early Archaic forms but are unrelated, being thousands of years later in time. The key is the small size, averaging 1-1/4 in. long. Sides are ex-curvate, the side notches low and rounded, notches and base areas well-ground, and base corners are squared to rounded. Oval in cross-section, these small pieces are fairly thick but well-chipped. Base edges tend to be straight or slightly excurvate. Possibly the dart-point version of Godar and Hemphill blades, this is not a common Ohio type. Flintridge, Indiana hornstone and Upper Mercer flints are frequently encountered in the Robin-son.

Ref. 58: p 327.

St. Albans
Variety A

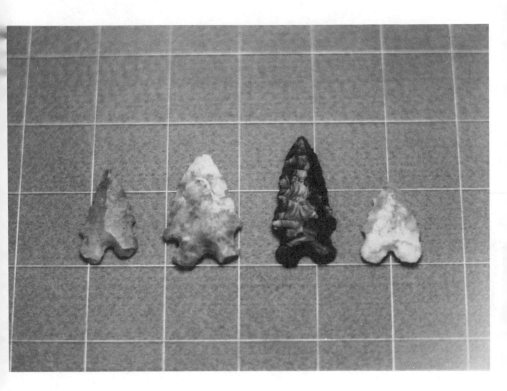

Triangular in outline, the Variety A is shorter and wider than Variety B, and shouldering is often better defined. Serrations were usually present, but may be all worn off one or both blade edges. Another knife form, Variety A has a large, broad base, rounded lobes, and a deep basal notch. The base area is well-ground. The type can be confusing when resharpening has removed the shoulders to the side notches, but the very triangular form persists. Dark flints and unusual lithics are common for Ohio specimens, these found usually on small, scattered Archaic sites and rarely in large quantities.

Ref. 6: pp 72-73. 16: p 1.

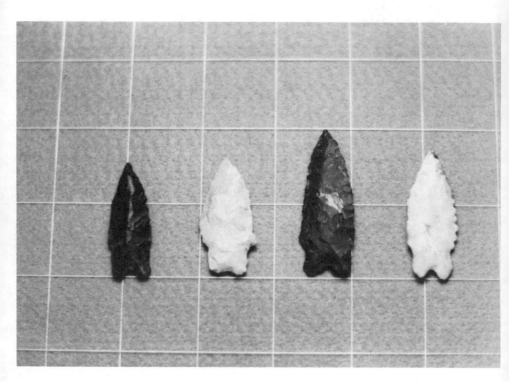

Related to the St. Albans Variety A, some Variety B's may be resharpened A's, now much more narrow. This type is long, with shallow side-notches and a typical bifurcated base. They are rechipped from both faces, giving some a lenticular cross-section. Light serrations are often present and it is widest at or just above the shoulders. Medium basal grinding is usually present. St. Albans Variety B was recovered from Zone 11 at St. Albans after Kirk Corner-notch and before LeCroy Bifurcated types.

Ref. 6: pp 74-75.

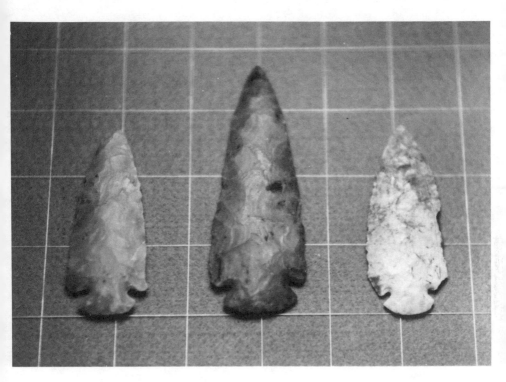

Long a favorite knife form for collectors due to size, excellent material, attractive configuration and superb workstyle, there is a wide variety of "Doves" in Ohio. All have the well-polished baseline, deep and narrow notching and, for many, eye-catching length. Ohio had at least half-a-dozen type varieties, summarized briefly below.

1. Standard-base, size well-matched to blade.
2. Large-base, or, with relatively high notching.
3. Small-base, with notches nearer the base than sides.
4. Fractured-base, with corners burin-flaked at 45 degrees.
5. True Notched-base form, usually a Standard sub-type.
6. Miniature forms, most 2 to 3 in. long.

Ref. 2: pp 102-103. 58: p 332.

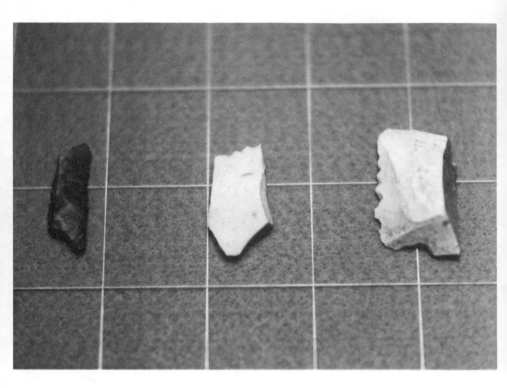

Possible also found in other cultural periods, Sawtooth (serrated-edge) Flakes are a minority tool type. While serrated hafted knives are common in the Early Archaic and serrated arrowheads in the Mississippian, these flakes are easy to overlook. Typical examples are made on the thinnest edge of the flake and (opposed to most blade-edging) are chipped in mainly from one side. Teeth vary in number from a few to nearly a dozen. Some teeth are not particulary sharp and most are no longer than 1/8 inch. The examples shown were picked up on Archaic and multi-component sites. Far fewer than one in a hundred worked flakes will have this edge treatment.

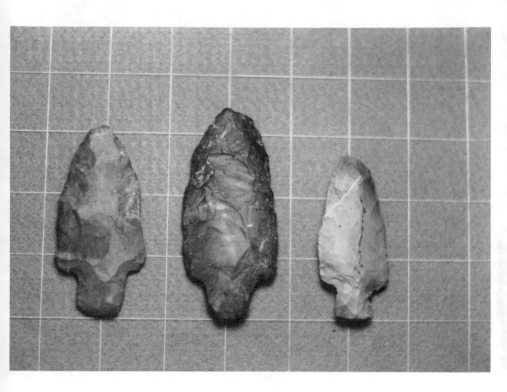

A long, thick stemmed piece, the Scherschel is often roughly made and somewhat crude in appearance. Shoulders are angular to rounded, and edges are excurvate. The stem is short for overall length, and may have moderate grinding, while the baseline is slightly convex. Stem sides may be straight, but some specimens expand at the base, giving a side-notched configuration. The Scherschel may have edge-dulling or broken tips, suggesting hard knife use. Cherts of all kinds were used for the type, some from unknown sources.

Ref. 58: p 345.

Resembling some Buzzard Roost Creek examples, this not un-common piece does not seem to be named in Ohio. Edges are ex-curvate, shoulders bold to mild depending on resharpening, but always somewhat rounded. The stem is broad, thin and short, tapering toward the base which is ground. The base corners are short and rounded, the basal indentation quite shallow. Blade faces are gently rounded and small serrations are sometimes present. Semi-bifurcates are extremely well-chipped, nicely re-touched and one lower face usually has flute-like basal thinning. Curiously, more than half of the specimens have one base corner broken. There are some similarities to the (probably unrelated) Heavy Duty for this type.

Ref. 58: p 57.

These are small stemmed pieces with serrated edges. They taper from thickest at the shoulders to thinnest at the tips, and serrations may be well-worn. The shoulders are angular, almost barbed, and the short stem is about 3/8 in. long and less than 1/2 in. wide. Stem sides are well-ground, but the stem base is lightly ground, if at all. Basal thinning of the stem is present, and some shoulder tips are fracture-chipped off. Despite their arrowhead-like appearance, knife-serrations and shoulder-fracturing suggest the Archaic, possibly Early.

One of a number of little-known types from Ohio's vast Archaic period, there is probably no relationship to the Weak-stemmed type despite a superficial resemblence. The Slight-stemmed has excurvate edges and is thick and lenticular in cross-section. The broad tapered stem is extremely short, the base sides gradually indented, and the basal edge is convex. Surprisingly for an Archaic origin (due to percussion-pressure chipping mix and materials) the basal region is only lightly ground. These are scarce pieces and few collections have many good examples. Dark flints were commonly used.

The Snapped-stem has a very short rounded stem that appears to be snapped off at an angle. The base may be part of an original break, or, is the original core surface. The stem bottom is angled closer to one face and the base-bottom break area may have some smoothing. Edges are excurvate to straight and shoulders are angular to barbed. An interesting feature is that one edge of the stem may have fracture-chipping. The less-angled (sharper) basal edge was sometimes used as a chipping platform for stem-thinning. The fracture-chipping, basal-edge grinding and lenticular blades suggest an Archaic placement.

Ref. 74.

This is a generalized knife form that apparently lasted for several centuries in the Archaic. The base is rounded, also base corners, and edges are excurvate to straight. Beveling is sometimes present, and usually stops short (see smaller photo example) of the base where handle attachment wrapped the edges. Most Stanfields are medium or large in size, thickest at center and tapering to the edges. Almost any of the many Ohio flints was used, both in-state and exotic, from elsewhere.

Ref. 58: p 360.

Another of the large bifurcate-base family, this type has a relatively small base for size. Edges are excurvate, shoulders rounded to angular, and thickest portion is at face center just above the shoulders. Almost stemmed, the base corners of the Stanly usually expand and bifurcation is not large or deep. There is often heavy grinding on the stem sides, less on base bottom center. Some tips are off-center due to unequal edge resharpening of this knife form, and serrations may be present on some pieces. In North Carolina, the Stanly was found with unfinished semilunar Atl-atl weights.

Ref. 56: p 21. 57: p 92. 58: p 361.

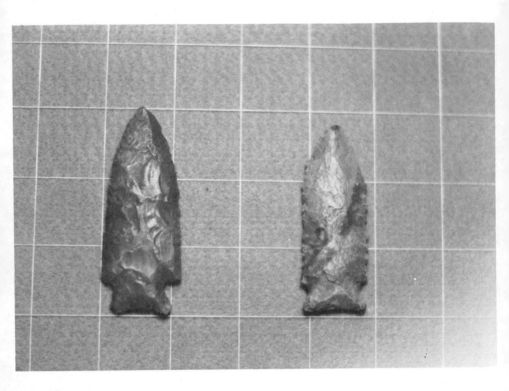

This is a long knife form, usually extremely well made. It is noted for regular serrations, when they are present, and the faces are fairly flat, edges thin. Corner-notched, the Stilwell has upswept notches, which on less-resharpened edges form shoulder barbs. The base bottom is incurvate and corners are rounded to pointed. The hafting area is ground, ranging from light to heavy. It greatly resembles a longer, thinner higher-notched Kirk Corner-notch (Large) from the same period. This is not a common type for Ohio; many examples are made from Indian hornstone.

Ref. 28: pp 56, 58, 87. 58: p 365.

While related hafted tool types exist (see Ground-edge Sha-pers), more common are medium to large flakes with one or more straight edges that are ground. Sometimes the edge is flat in relation to flake body, but it may be angled slightly, one edge higher. Often that edge (or either or both edges) will have some degree of dulling about midway from the ends. Apparently this is from use-wear, probably woodworking for which these would have ideal non-hafted planes. In a few cases the straight edge is angled to provide a very strong tip, which itself may show heavy use.

Usually large, these knives all have one very unusual characteristic. Base corners are rounded, or angled, the base straight unless damaged or worn, the side-notches deep. The base-line is lightly ground, notches moderately ground. The Stressed-blade is widest at the shoulders and basal thinning is present. The key is the blade which is not in line with the base, but twisted up or down. (To visualize, imagine that the flint was plastic and the base, and blade near the tip, were given a slight twist in opposite directions.) These are not beveled but were purpose-made in this strange fashion. Material, design, workstyle and find-circumstances all suggest the Archaic.

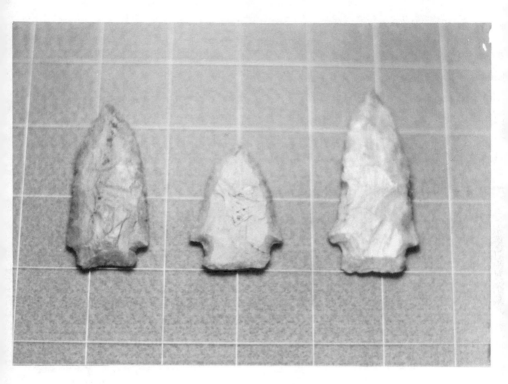

Associated with the Big Sandy component at the Eva Site in
Tennessee, the Sykes is found with some frequency in Ohio.
Fairly thick, the faces are flat, the edges of this knife form
resharpened equally from both sides. The notches characteristic-
ally are small, squared and set in the corners. Resharpened edges
went only to the shoulder tips, which may eventually project out
from the blade. Base bottoms are straight to slightly incurvate,
and are ground. Ohio specimens are often made of a light brown
flint or chert.

Ref. 40: pp 40, 42, 45.

While the collector name is descriptive, the type looks more like a Greek amphora in profile. Edges are always excurvate, the base straight or excurvate. These are very carefully made, the edges and faces evidencing fine pressure retouching that gives a smooth appearance. The base has large notches which create an expanded stem. Base bottoms are moderately ground, while the entire notch area—base corners to shoulder tips—is heavily ground, removing all sharp edges. The tip of some Table Rock pieces is angled or canted to one side. Any good grade of flint was used for Ohio specimens.

Ref. 33: pp 8-9. 78: pp 15-16.

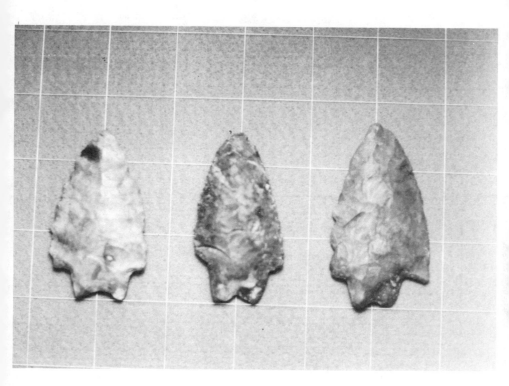

Very similar to the Lawrence Broad-blade to which it may be related, the Tapered-stem Bifurcate has a short base and rounded indentation that creates bifurcation. Stem sides are medium-ground, base bottoms less so. The distinguishing feature is the angled face, with the obverse or front normal, the reverse or back-side flat or angled. Made from large, flat curved flakes, this angles the whole blade toward the reverse. These knives are fairly large, yet thin. The reverse may have large percussion flake scars, completely different from that of the front.

Ref. 11: p 37.

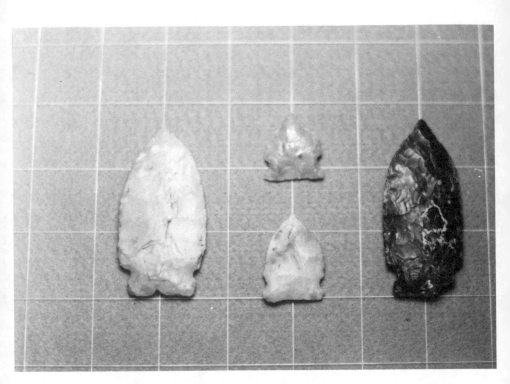

These scarce knives are readily identifed. Overall they are wide for length, have straight bases and fairly shallow side notches set low on the blade. The base-line has light to moderate grinding, while notches are heavily ground. The key is the small tip, formed when the sides abruptly converge and then extend. Most examples are heavy in cross-section, but like most Archaic pieces are extremely well chipped. Taper-tips may be related to other Early Archaic types that are also side-notched. Flintridge and Upper Mercer flints predominate.

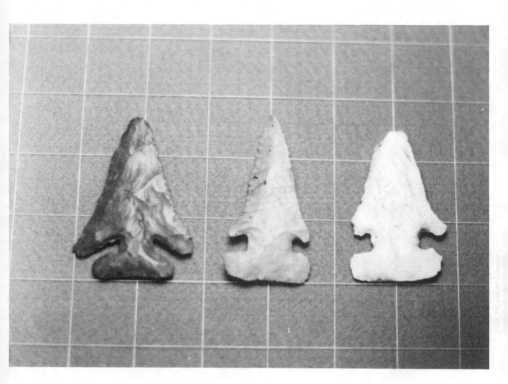

The type had also been called "Expanded-notch" and "Key-notch", these names and "E-notch" all referring to the identifying notch. This is a large knife form, often beveled or serrated, with well-ground straight or excurvate bases. The blade is triangular and edges may be incurvate after heavy resharpening, while basal lobes are rounded. Basal grinding is present. The narrow side notches abruptly widen and a small projection remains. A few examples may be more nearly corner- than side-notched. The entire wide range of Early Archaic flints was employed for the E-notch.

Ref. 1: pp 20-21. 10: p 26. 58: p 377.

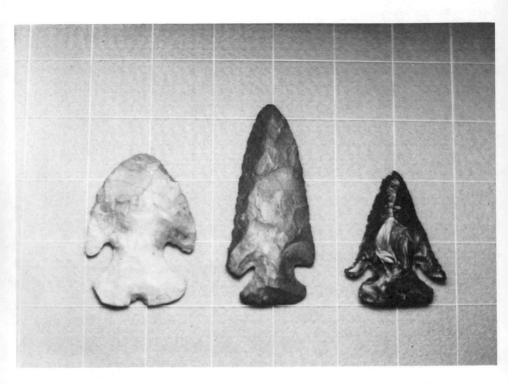

Limited to the Ohio area and nearby regions to the South and West, this knife form has a compressed distribution. The face is fairly flat and all resharpened examples have beveling. The base is straight, base corners rounded, and notching is deep and upswept in a graceful curve. The basal edges are ground, usually heavily. Some examples have very narrow stems which resulted in breakage, while other worn-down blades were made into drills. Many kinds of Ohio flints were used for this fairly scarce blade type.

Ref. 58: p 378.

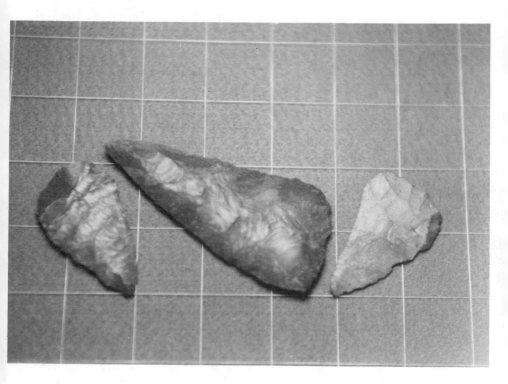

This small knife form is distinctive, yet not frequently found. The base is irregular, roughly formed with large percussion flake scars and little edge retouch. The backing or secondary edge is excurvate to straight, unretouched. The working edge is excurvate to incurvate and may be shallowly beveled. A key is the very delicate ribbon-like flaking on this edge, and scars may extend some distance across the flat faces. Extremely thin in cross-section, the type is often made of good grades of tan flint. Overall design and superb edge-treatment suggest an Archaic placement despite the lightly ground base.

This is a minor Ohio artifact type, identified by the very short, wide stem. It is quite narrow in cross-section, with flat faces. Edges are excurvate until being resharpened, and they terminate at the shoulders, the widest portion. Shoulder tips are rounded to angular. Base sides are generally straight but may flare toward the base, or, body. The baseline is fairly straight and there is basal thinning consisting of wide, flat flakes. Basal grinding is present. An almost identical type in Alabama is called the White Springs. Dark Ohio flints were usually used in this state.

Ref: 7: p 14. 11: p 41. 75: p 44.

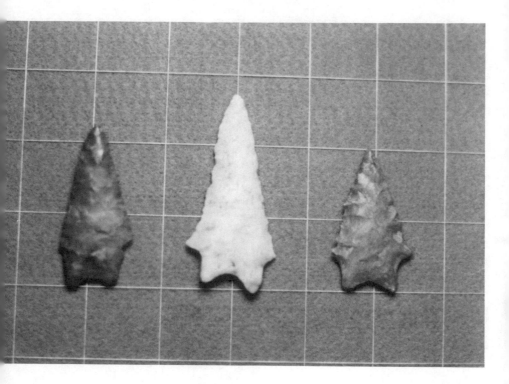

Sometimes mis-identified as the Kirk-stemmed, the Wide-base is more likely related to the Tapered-stem. While it also has a stem which contracts toward the base, it lacks a pronounced ''bent'' blade. The Wide-base is much narrower on average and is widest at the shoulders. It is thickest just above the jutting shoulders and tapers toward the tip. Usually serrated, the Wide-base has a very broad, heavily ground base and base sides. The bifurcated base is sharply incurvate. Often one or both shoulders may be fracture-chipped off, the sign of knife use in Ohio's Early Archaic.

These have rounded bases and excurvate sides, overall a pleasing leaf-like outline. Faces are flat, and there is little basal-area grinding. In most cases, highest-grade Flintridge jewel variety flint was used. While some may have served as-is for knife use, it is probable also that some are preforms for various stemmed Adena blades. (A variety has a less rounded basal edge, more like the Hopewell triangular knife, a blending form.) Nine Cache Blades 3 to 4 inches long were found in the original Adena Mound on the Worthington estate during excavations in 1901.

Ref. 13: p 108. 44: p 469. 46: p 132. 77: pp 82-83.

Directly related to Adena Cache Blades — and sometimes found with burials in mounds — this blade type is yet distinctive. There are two sub-types. One is a thinner version of the classic Cache Blade, and when stemmed produced a rounded stem base. The second has a very slightly convex base (almost straight) and when stemmed produced a straight stem base. The two differ mainly in degree of basal roundness and one type may blend with the other. They are distinguished from similar Archaic types due to slightly inferior workstyle, lack of basal grinding, and the absence of strong beveling.

Ref. 13: p 108. 23: p 39. 43: p 164. 45: p 259.

Long so-called because the diminutive size was thought suitable for birds, these in fact appear to be general-purpose dart-tips or arrowheads. True Birdpoints are an inch or less in length, fairly wide, and may be corner- or side-notched. Chipping on some is superb, while on others it is poorly done. A few are made from broken points or knives, the break still evident on the base bottom. Notching in most cases is fairly delicate. Though all Ohio cultures produced extra-small specimens now and then, Birdpoints as described are indeed a separate type. They have been found on sites producing Hopewell cores and bladelets. Flintridge is a common material.

Ref. 39: pp 11-15.

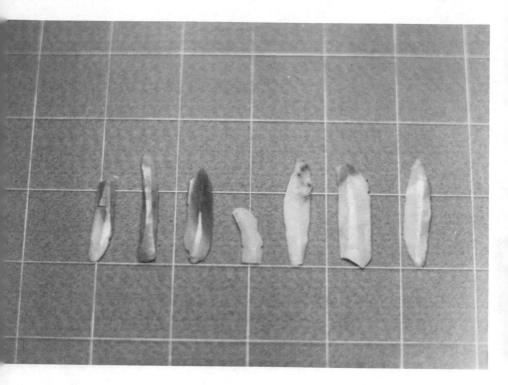

The easiest-to-recognize of all chipped artifacts, these long, slender and very thin pieces are yet easy to overlook in the field. Struck from the parent block (see Core), they average just under 1-1/2 in. in length, are 1/4 to 1/2 in. wide, and 1/8 to 1/16 in. thick. The excurvate face usually shows the scars of previous strike-offs, while the incurvate reverse is smooth. At times, fine secondary chipping is present. Some examples have edges lightly ground at the punch-struck end for a distance of about 3/8 inches, indicating a haft for these tiny knives. A few pieces may have small notches near the same end. In Ohio, Flintridge was the preferred material.

Ref. 32: p 10-11.

This is one of the easiest to recognize of all unhafted knife forms. It has an excurvate baseline, and edges are straight or a bit excurvate. Chipping is nearly the best of Woodland times, being a fine mix of primary and secondary, giving the blades a beautiful, well-finished appearance. Most Cache Blades-Classic are quite thin and fairly flat in cross-section. Found in mounds or on village sites or individually, these blades resemble Hopewell pieces without notching. (A more ovate form is called the North, 100 BC-AD 350). Base areas are not ground. Jewel-quality Flintridge was often used, and may have been the preferred material.

Ref. 11: p 60. 23: pp 38-39. 42: pp 156-157, 216-217. 58: p 275.

Less common than the Classic, this blade has also been found in mounds and on village sites. It differs from the Classic in having a straight or slightly concave base and many examples are extensively shouldered, giving the pentagonal appearance. The shoulder may be longer on one base edge than the other, and may extend for half the overall length. High-grade materials are not as frequent for this type, which averages 3 in. long. While there is some similarity to other unhafted knife forms, the Pentagonal has longer shouldering than the Ft. Ancient, and is not as thin as Jack's Reef blades.

Ref. 11: p 60. 42: pp 154-155.

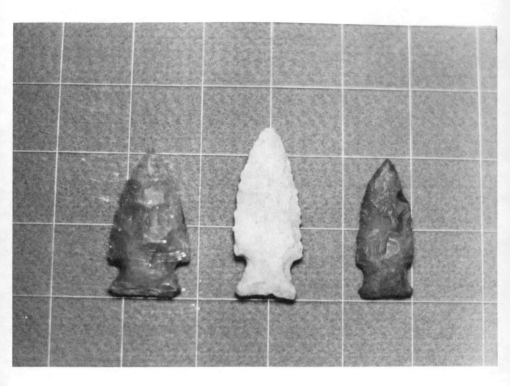

Found on Cole Complex sites and in several rock-shelter excavations (Peters; Raven Rocks), the Chesser-notched types
began in the Middle Woodland and ended by Ft. Ancient times. It
has Woodland-like notching, being low and shallow, and deeper
at the top than bottom. The typical Chesser is long and fairly narrow, with excurvate edges. The stem expands at the base, and
basal corners are pointed or rounded, the shoulders small. An
identification key is the straight baseline, which differentiates
some earlier Hopewell pieces with the excurvate baseline. The
basal area is unground. Local charts and flints were dominant for
the type.

Ref. 53: p 22. 58: p 73. 64: pp 21-22, 54. 66: pp 26-28.

Convex-edge Knives*

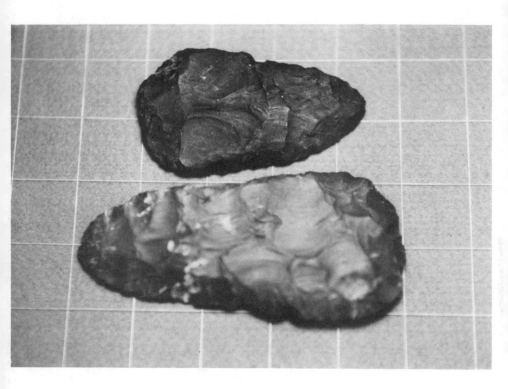

While some of these pieces may be last-stage preforms for Cache Blades-Classic, they seem to be a close family type. As the name implies, all edges are excurvate. Many examples are larger than true Classic blades, and lack the very careful facial treatment and edge retouch. Some examples do not have extremely pointed tips, these perhaps wear-dulled. Many Convex-edge Hopewell Knives have edge rechipping and break-repairs, showing actual use. Bases are thinned for hafting, and remain unground. Resharpening may straighten base sides. Black Ohio flints were often used.

Ref. 23: pp 38-39.

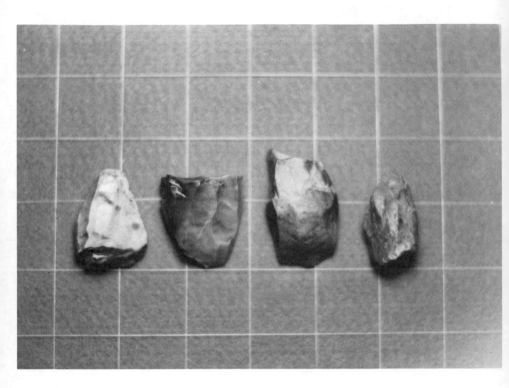

While basic flint blocks in one form or another were used for striking off blades in all prehistoric Ohio periods, the word Cores usually refers to Hopewell pieces. Further, the classic Hopewellian core was made from multicolored Flintridge material. These are irregular flint masses with one side worked flat or scooped to provide a striking platform to detach long, thin bladelets. This was done by indirect percussion. While large and unstruck core blanks exist, most bear the scars of multiple bladelet removals. Some are nearly exhausted. The cores are found on any site where there was Hopewell Indian activity, and many have come from on or near the Flintridge quarries in Licking County.

Ref. 46: pp 137, 140-141. 58: pp 8-9.

With ancestors in the Late Archaic, the Cresap is an Early Adena type that exists in several forms. Both are fairly large and sturdy; one is wide, with a wide stem, while the other is more narrow in both dimensions. Both have a similar stem. The Cresap tapers from rounded shoulders to a straight base and stem sides may be lightly ground, the baseline the same. Named after a West Virginia mound, the Cresap is sometimes found with a straight-stemmed type. Size and edge retouch on some specimens suggests use as knives, and a range of quality flints was used.

Ref. 13: p 110. 51: pp 128-129, 154. 58: p 91.

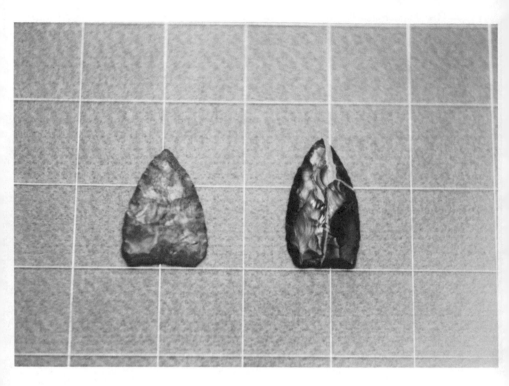

Except for the incurvate base, the Frazier's thinned base looks very much like a preform for several of the late Woodland types. Edges are excurvate, the base incurvate, and shoulders pointed or rounded by rechipping. These are extremely well-made artifacts, being very thin and with further basal thinning on most examples. The wide form suggests knife use and resharpening shortens and narrows the top. There is little or no side or basal grinding. The Frazier is longer, wider and thinner than most points of the period. High-grade flints were used for most examples.

Ref. 38: p 83. 58: p 137.

Hopewell Arrowheads

Woodland
Hopewell

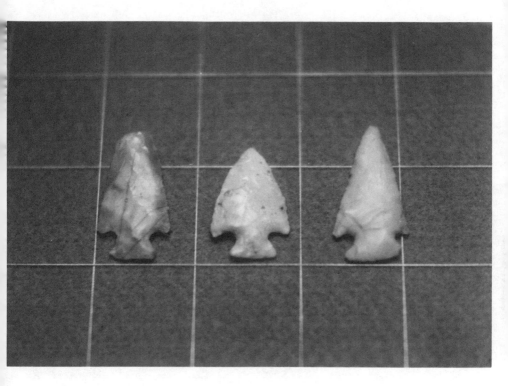

Averaging 1-1/4 in. long, these fine small points should not be confused with Birdpoints. The latter tend to be shorter, wider and less well-made. True Hopewell Arrowheads have been found on sites that also contained typical Hopewell corner-notches, cores and bladelets. Most Arrowheads are corner-notched and made of high high-grade Flintridge, often glossy and colorful. Chipping is above average, notching deep to create an expanded base, and there is little or no basal grinding. Some Hopewell Arrowheads seem to copy in miniature the larger points/blades, maintaining design for a new weapon.

Ref. 8: p 15.

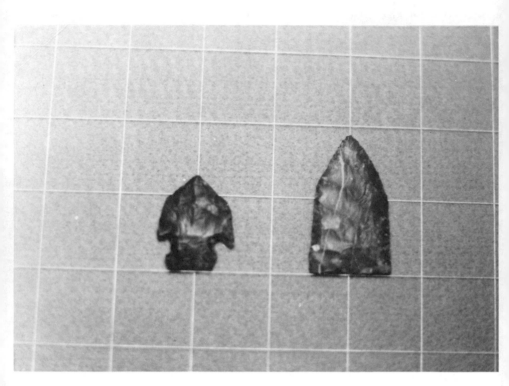

Jack's Reef points, arrowheads and knives, are of two sub-types: Corner-notched, and Pentagonal. Both are small, very thin and with exquisite pressure-chipping overall. Notches come in from corners or lower sides and are usually deep, often upswept in a curved fashion. Basal grinding (light) is present on perhaps half these pieces. Base corners and shoulder tips may be very barbed. The Pentagonal form is the same except for a sharply angled tip, and unnotched examples may be preforms or unhafted knives. Mills excavated examples at Mound City, Ohio. Grey, tan and white flints are common.

Ref. 69: pp 26-27, 28. 81: pp 18-19.

One of the early true arrowheads, the Klunk Side-notched is about an inch long and has wide side-notches close to the base corners. The unground base bottom is straight to slightly excurvate; shoulders and base corners are pointed. Stems may be fairly wide or quite narrow. A distinguishing feature of the Klunk is the flat area on one or both faces, part of the original flake from which it was fashioned. Klunk points are not uncommon in Ohio, yet very few are found on the typical multicomponent site. Photo examples are all from Wayne County.

Ref. 58: p 209.

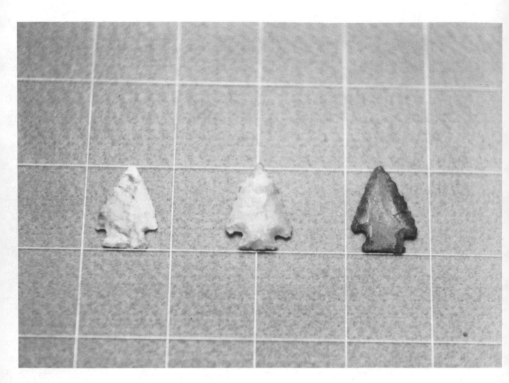

What most people call "arrowheads", for once the term is correct. The Koster Corner-notch has excurvate edges, strong barbed shoulders and large rounded notches. The stem averages 3/8 in. wide and base corners are tipped, the base straight to slightly excurvate. Unusual for such a late piece, there is extensive basal grinding, at times up to the shoulders. Oval in cross-section, many of these pieces were made from a large flake and the large original facets may remain. (Two of the illustrated examples have this trait on the reverse.) Flintridge is known for Ohio examples.

Ref. 58: p 211.

With excurvate edges and pronounced shouldering, this type could resemble many other stemmed examples. However, the stem itself is rectangular, has squared base corners and the stem sides are heavily ground. Grinding extends to the lower portion of the shoulders. The stem edges and base are always straight, and the stem is usually two-fifths the total length. Some of the lesser-known flints have been used for the type.

Ref. 58: p 212.

This is one of several triangular true arrowheads (arrival of bow, AD 500-AD 800, Ohio region) found in the state. Edges are straight to incurvate, the base always incurvate in a gradual line, or angled to the point center. Basal dimensions in some examples are almost as wide as length, and corners may be almost as pointed as the tip. Most Levannas are well-made, though crude examples exist. Some are much larger than those shown and may have served as knives; local cherts and flints were widely used. This type may be related to the similar Yadkin of the Carolinas.

Ref. 58: p 226. 69: pp 31-32.

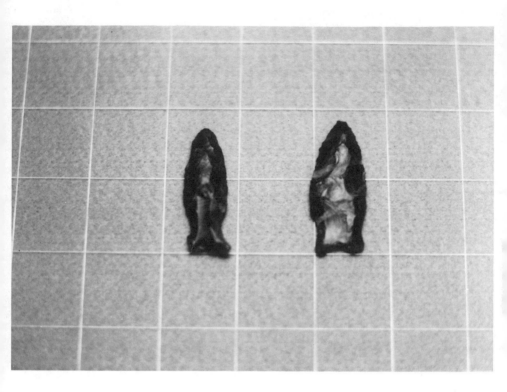

Also known as the Orient Fishtail after the New York type, these are found with some regularity on Ohio sites. It presents a narrow appearance, is fairly thick, and averages just under 2 in. long. The base has long, shallow basal indentations that form a stem. The basal corners have projecting ears that usually do not go past the sloping shoulders, and the base is straight or incurvate. Basal grinding is present. Not to be confused with the Fishspear, the Orient Fishtail is stemmed instead of notched, is eared, and often has a concave base. A number of examples have come from Ohio rockshelters.

Ref. 5: pp 60-61. 58: p 281. 64: p 321. 69: p 39.

As with the somewhat similar Jack's Reef, this is a small arrowhead or knife, delicately pressure-flaked, thin, with flat faces. The type is side-notched, the notches rather squared, with rounded terminals. The notching is usually exactly opposite and the configuration does not allow shoulder barbs. About half will have light basal grinding. The type can be distinguished from Jack's Reef because of notch placement and basal corners, which are large and squared. Grey, tan and white flints predominate.

Ref. 11: p 65. 81: pp 19-21.

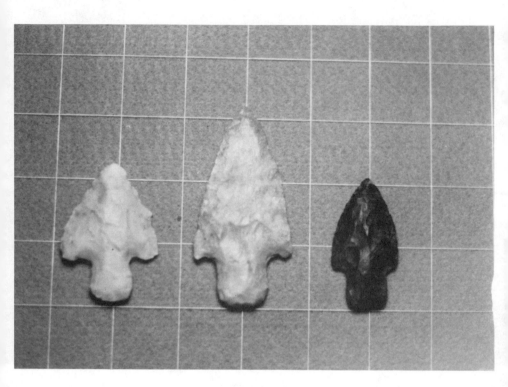

Very similar to the Squared-stem, this Robbins form has excurvate edges and strong, wide shouldering. The sturdy stem may contract slightly adjacent to the body, and stem sides are mainly straight. Base bottom is straight to convex, and basal corners are rounded. Faces are fairly flat and chipping tends to be above-average for Woodland blades of the stemmed design. The Robbins Rounded-stem was sometimes used as burial inclusions, especially large, fine pieces. Material from Coshocton County and Flintridge was preferred and white flint is often seen.

Ref. 13: p 112. 31: pp 10-11. 51: pp 139, 189. 58: p 326.

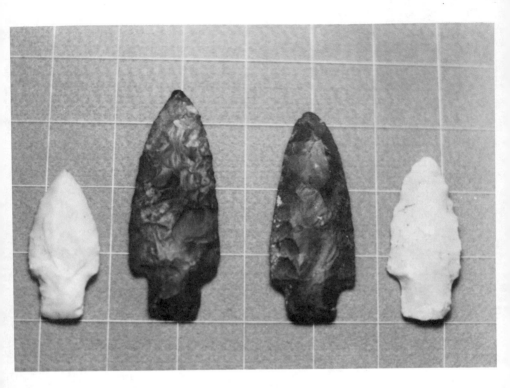

A robust yet well-made artifact, the Robbins has excurvate edges and is thick in cross-section. It is widest at the shoulders even after resharpening and is usually twice the width of the sturdy stem. The stem has straight sides and may be rectangular or taper gently toward the base. The base bottom is straight or slightly convex. Grinding on stem sides is usually present, and it may be heavy on the base bottom. Blade edges are usually carefully retouched; some Robbins base corners are rounded. Flintridge and Coshocton flints are most common.

Ref. 11: p 57. 13: p 114. 58: p 326.

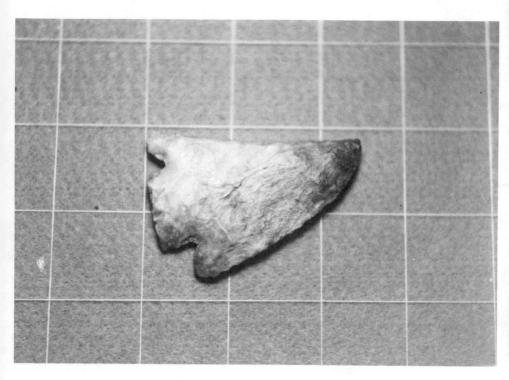

Ross pieces are large ceremonial blades that were found in Ross County, Ohio, Hopewell mounds. There is a wide variety of forms, of which only a small example (a #2) is shown. Types:
1. Stemmed, concavo-convex edges, straight blade.
2. Stemmed, excurvate and incurvate edges, curved blade.
3. Unnotched, extruded "V"-shaped wide baseline.
4. Unnotched, straight and wide baseline.
Variations on the above are known. Certain materials were used: Obsidian, Kaolin chert, Knife River flint and one or two others. Many of the large Ross Ceremonial blades were purposely broken or fire-cracked and must be reassembled from pieces.

Ref. 4: p 42. 48: pp 346-347. 58: p 329. 63: pp 51-52.

One of the best-known Ohio flints, Snyders points and knives are medium-large in size. The large notches are low on the sides, while the base bottom is slightly excurvate and lightly ground. Large pieces have fairly flat faces, while more narrow examples may be fairly thick in cross-section. Most Snyders are widest at the shoulders, the base the same width. Heavily resharpened specimens must be identified by thickness and the remains of notch interior configuration. Coshocton County and Flintridge materials were used, especially the latter for Ohio.

Ref. 5: pp 62-63. 11: p 59. 58: p 358. 69: p 49.

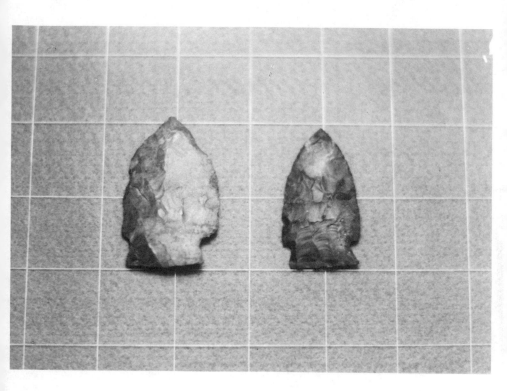

The Steuben has excurvate edges, a quite pointed tip and small, barbed shoulders that appear angular or rounded when the barbs are removed. Stems are an inch or more wide, the low notches are shallow and create sharp stem corners. The base is straight and notches may be ground more than the baseline. This is probably a knife form from Middle and Late Woodland times, and the keys are a wide, flat piece with fairly sharp edges all around. Related to the Chesser, dark flints and various cherts predominate for the Steuben.

Ref. 58: p 363.

Possibly a Northern version of the Sublet Ferry, edges are excurvate, shoulders sharp but not barbed, and notches are very
low. (This is an example of notch placement so low that side-
notching and corner-notching may merge.) Notches are rounded,
the stem is about half the width of the shoulders, and base corners are pointed. The baseline is straight and lightly ground.
Blades are larger than some similar Brewerton Side-notches, the
edges are more excurvate, and the base proportionately smaller.
Base corners may be broken or worn, altering the appearance.
Dark flints, glacial cobbles and Indiana Green flints have been
seen for the type.

Ref. 58: p 366.

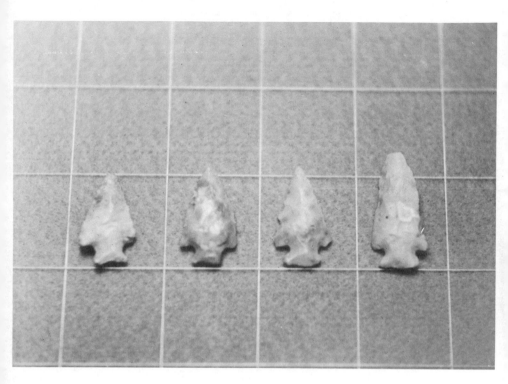

These small points are thick in cross-section and have well-defined, almost barbed shoulders. The corner-notching is deep and rounded, sometimes giving the base a stemmed appearance. The base is always less wide than the shoulders, and the base-bottom is only lightly ground, the notches more so. Averaging just over 1-¼ in. long, most examples have extremely pointed tips. These are not over-size Birdpoints. High-quality glossy flints were used, especially Flintridge, and most are well-made. Find-circumstances, material, size and configuration suggest a Hopewell affiliation and they are probably true arrowheads.

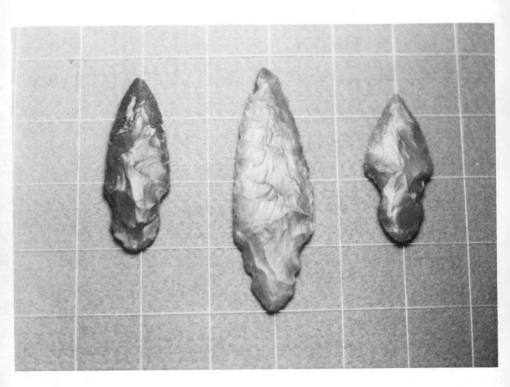

Turkeytails, so-called by collectors from the shape of the hafting stem, have excurvate sides and are bipointed. The more pointed end is the tip, the less pointed the haft area. Most Turkeytails have small rounded side-notches and the resultant stem is slightly less-wide than the shoulders. Ohio has three types and two sub-types. The Fulton is wide and may have a recurved tip. The Harrison is longer in comparison and less-wide. The Hebron is similar to the Harrison, but more nearly stemmed than notched. Hebron sub-types are one with a stem that is also notched, and, a barbed-shoulder variety. Turkeytails are often found in caches, and the near-universal material is Indiana hornstone, also known as Harrison County flint, Dongola flint or Golconda chert.

Ref. 29: pp 146-147. 58: pp 141, 173, 177.

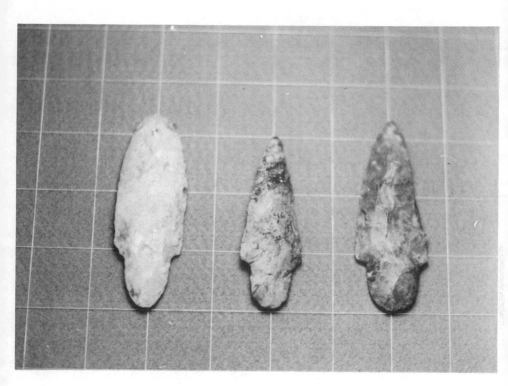

More often found North and West of the state, the Waubesa occasionally turns up in Ohio. It can be distinguished from the more common Adena by the base. Bases are an inch or less wide at the top of the stem and taper to a rounded base. This base may be almost pointed, giving a certain double-tipped appearance to the piece. Stems are lightly ground on the edges and shoulders are angular but never barbed. These tend to be fairly large, and made from any flints utilized by the Middle Woodland Indians.

Ref. 58: p 393. 72: p 40.

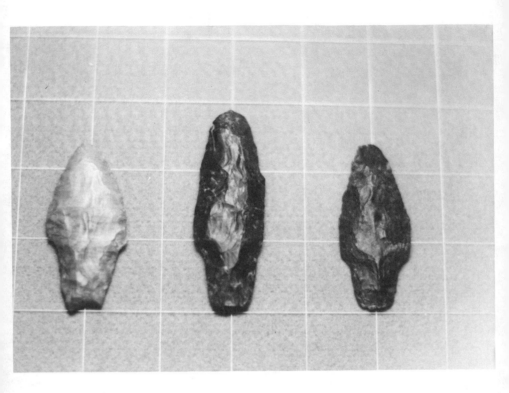

Probably ancestral to the more widespread Adena types, these artifacts often have use-damage or heavy wear. They are long and narrow, and the shoulders are not pronounced. The stem is long and tapers gently to the base, itself usually excurvate. The stem is heavily ground to the shoulders. Some specimens appear to be rather quickly or crudely made. Upper Mercer flints from Coshocton deposits is common, but any type flint used in the period can be expected. Some early investigators termed these drills, but most are more likely heavily used knife forms.

Ref. 11: p 53. 13: p 143.

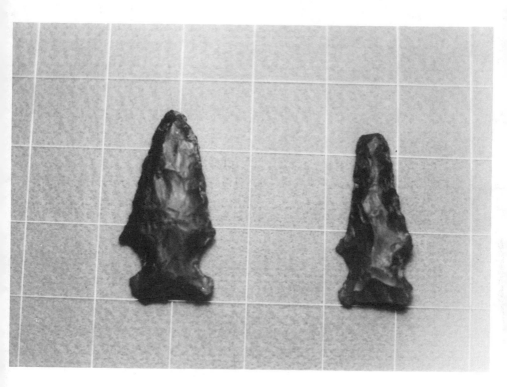

While this type has some resemblance to various Hopewell types, it is yet distinctive. The base is straight to irregular, corners angular to rounded, and the base is about the same width as the shoulders. Probably knive forms, many are quite thick from frequent resharpening. Flaking is irregular but well-done, and bases may have some thinning. Base and notches, however, are not ground and retain their sharp original edges. For size, notches are extremely long or wide for any prehistoric artifact type. The wide notching suggests heavy hafting arrangements, typical of knife use.

This Hopewell sub-type is very unusual and exists only in small numbers. It is similar to the main Snyders type except it has only the single notch. The opposite, unnotched edge is usually straight or a bit excurvate. There it has no shoulder, or only a slight protrusion as a hafting aid. Due to the relative thickness of the unnotched side it is highly possible that these are not special-made curiosities, but typical knives that had one edge resharpened until the notch merged with edge, leaving a single opposite notch. They are found as scattered strays on Hopewell sites.

Ref. 53: pp 21-23.

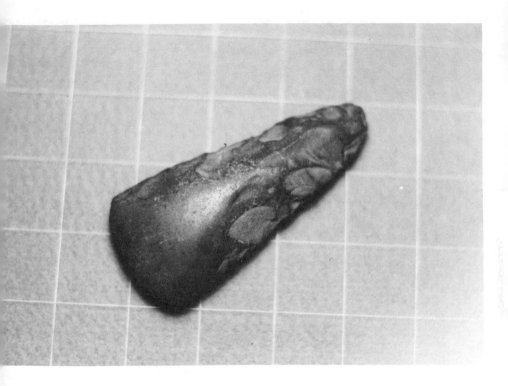

The Ft. Ancient peoples used two kinds of chipped flint celts. Type A (Author's designation) was fairly rough and unfinished, and averaged perhaps 4-½ in. long. Type B (shown) was highly finished. The entire lower blade area was polished, with special attention paid to the cutting edge. The preliminary form was rough-chipped into basic shape by percussion. Also related to Ft. Ancient are other polished flint celt-like artifacts, including adzes, chisels and gouges. For the most part, locally available cherts were utilized and the use of high-quality materials such as Flintridge is rare. Polished flint celts are usually found in southern Ohio.

Ref. 22: pp 147, 153, 162. 37: pp 58-59.

These knives tend to have straight sides and a triangular outline. While some Ft. Ancient knives are notched the more common form is a blade with a squared base. Knife lower edges are parallel for a short length, for hafting accomodation, before reverting to the normal triangular form. Basal grinding, if present, is slight and chipping tends to be average-good. Cherts and flints of many local deposits were used, plus some Flintridge. The base line is fairly straight and may be slightly angled. The Baum Site had several Ft. Ancient knife forms.

Ref. 22: pp 71, 94, 122 plate XXXI.

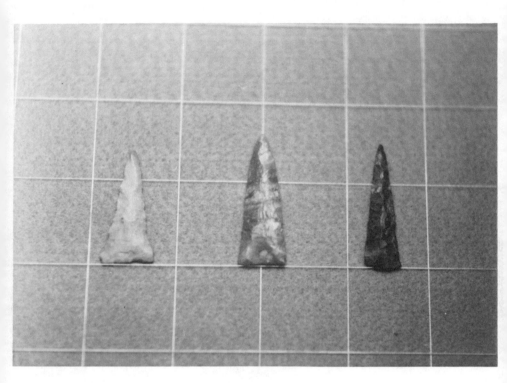

Almost identical to the Ft. Ancient-Serrated point, some non-serrated or Plain points may have insipient serrations, very faintly put in. The Plain type appears to be slightly shorter and a bit wider than Serrated examples, but in the latter case serrations make more narrow-looking faces. Base bottoms are identical to Serrated examples. Most of these triangles are quite well made and sometimes the chipping is excellent. Surface-finds from minor Ft. Ancient sites are often fragmentary and the signs are that such damage was from heavy or long-term use. Local flints or cherts were widely used.

Ref. 19: p 48. 45: p 369.

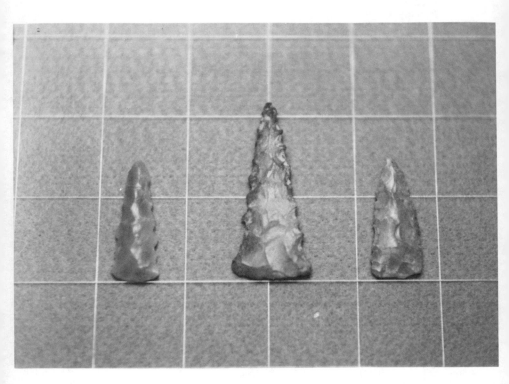

This is "the" Ft. Ancient point, large numbers of which (true arrowheads) were found at the five-acre Feurt Site, Scioto County, Ohio. These points are triangular, narrow, and some have large serrations for size. The base is usually straight, but may be slightly excurvate or incurvate. Feurt produced over a thousand examples, about half Serrated, half non-serrated or Plain. Some notched and some stemmed points were also found, and these too are of course Ft. Ancient types.

Ref. 22: pp 70-71. 45: p 368.

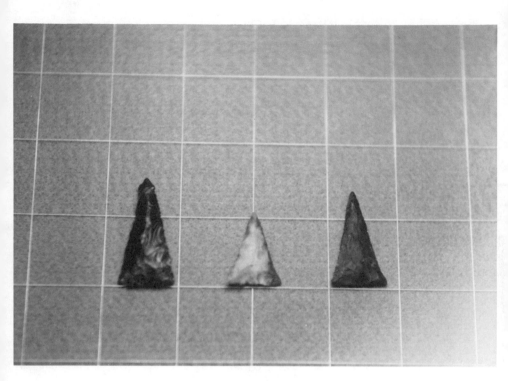

This true arrowhead point type was named in Illinois and a few examples are found in Ohio. The base is 3/5 as wide as length, edges are straight to a bit incurvate while the base is straight or a bit incurvate or excurvate. They tend to be wider at the base than similar unserrated examples of Ft. Ancient--Plain. Madisons have a less "ragged" baseline, and incurvate edges. Overall, they appear to be somewhat better made. There is often a confusing blending of types in overlap regions causing difficulty in firmly placing the types.

Ref. 5: p 68. 19: p 48. 58: p 236. 69: pp 33-34.

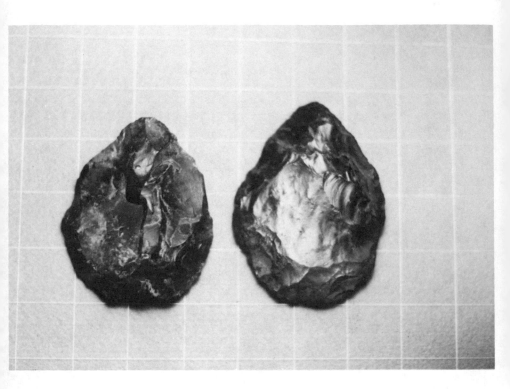

Blanks are unfinished flint masses, preforms for completed artifacts. They range from very rough quarry blocks to semi-
finished pieces that lack only basal features, and perhaps some
edge retouching. Blanks have been found on or near major Ohio
quarries, at village sites, in mounds, and as underground
deposits or caches. When not associated with burials or
ceremonial earthworks, the pieces may have been buried for
safekeeping or as stores of items for trade. Most Blanks are
thick, irregular, and largely percussion-flaked. The example
photographed on right has an old label on the reverse, ''Con-
gress, Ohio, 1903''.

The flint Chopper is generally so simple, even crude, that it is usually not diagnostic for any one culture. They are found in some degree and in some form in all prehistoric Ohio periods. Most are fairly large, and it is one of the few flint artifacts that may not have had a handle. One long side is usually percussion-flaked into a thick, strong edge, and the bulk of the piece can best be described as hand-sized. Many examples show hard use. This simple tool may have been used for dismembering large game, chopping food, or even for woodworking tasks like peeling bark.

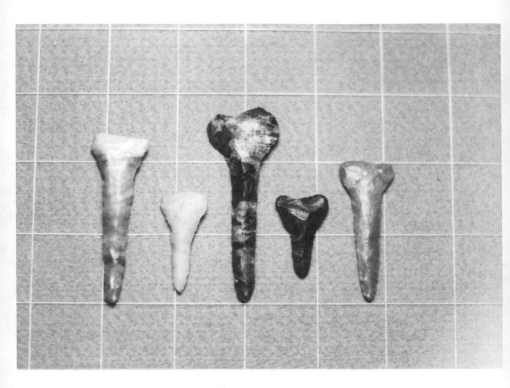

Variously called T-drills, flared- or expanded-base drills, these are a fairly common Ohio type. They began in Late Paleo times, possibly before, and such early examples may be 3 or more inches long. The haft or basal end is greatly or gently widened. There are many drill-base configurations, ranging from angular to squared to rounded. Like Pin drills, many Flared examples were probably made from worn-out blades, though some obviously were purpose-made from large flakes. The Archaic period has by far the largest number of such drills, and the greatest variety of lengths, basal shapes, materials, and so forth.

Ref. 12: pp 162-163. 30: p 38. 47: p 432 fig. 2. 62: p 38. 76: pp 256-258.

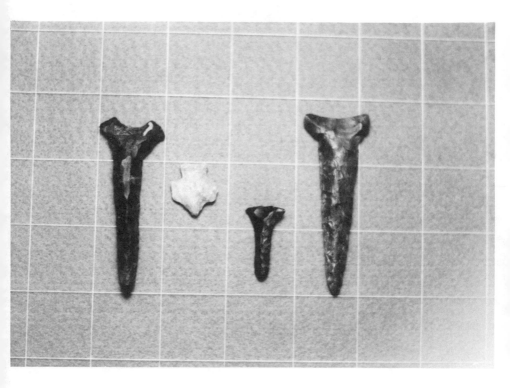

Type drills are those made from damaged or worn-out blades or points. They have bases sufficiently intact to identify the artifact types. Another class consists of drills with the basal section only (no notches) so that the type is difficult to pinpoint but the time-period can usually be identified. Type drills may have the base, notches and some shouldering, as, the much-admired St. Charles (Dovetail) drill. Period drills might have the base below the notches intact and a concave, well-ground baseline, indicating an Early Archiac placement. There are more Type drills than Flared, and more Flared drills than Pin-shaped.

Ref. 30: p 37.

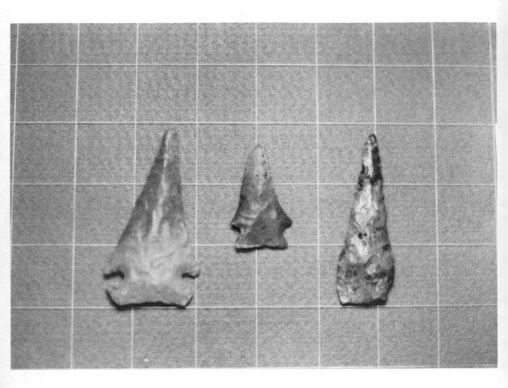

In numbers, Exhausted Blades are mainly Archaic, because of the 7000-year timespan. They are simply knives that were so frequently resharpened that cutting efficiency lessened and they were probably discarded. Characteristics of Exhausted Blades include: Very short blade length, sharply angled bevels, or blade narrow and/or thick in cross-section. Upon reaching this worn-out stage, the knives could be used as awls or perforators, be rechipped as drills or scrapers, or be discarded. Some have the so-called "impact fluting" at the tip, this usually purposely done to thin the blade tip for further use.

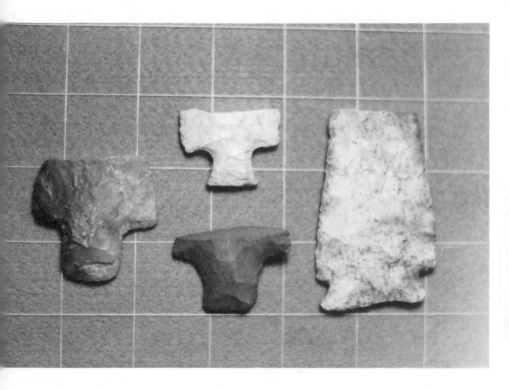

This unusual artifact class apparently began as a broken knife or point, the break area being anywhere on the blade but usually near the base. This break was then ground down to a flat surface, this plane being slightly tilted to one edge or slightly angled toward one face, or both. The ground-down area became the working portion, and usually one or both long edges will have use-wear to some degree. The long and strong edge would have been ideal for working or shaping wood, hence the name. These are not common artifacts, and exist from Paleo to Mississippian times, though they are found most often in the Archaic.

Ref. 29: p 127.

Flint hammerstones, like their hardstone namesakes, are found in all Ohio prehistoric periods. Most have rounded surfaces, often with signs of battering, and lack grooves for hafting. Lower grades of flint and chert were often used, perhaps reserving better grades for other artifacts. And, while a wide size variation exists, many can be comfortably held in the fingers of one hand. Hammerstones were used for several different purposes. Some were used with direct percussion to chip flint, or for indirect percussion (with bone or antler punch), while others may have been used with cupstones in food preparation. Still others, especially beginning about the Middle Archaic, were used to shape hardstone and slate artifacts.

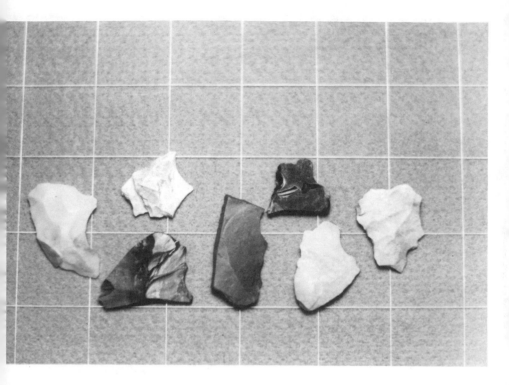

While these miniature tool forms have been found on sites ranging from Paleo to Mississippian, they seem to be found most frequently on those from Archaic times. Extremely simple, they have one or more rounded concave depressions formed on the edge(s) of a percussion-made flake. These areas usually were not chip-begun, but were simply worn into the edge through use. Some few do have minor pressure retouches. Apparently these are shaft-smoothing mini-tools, readily made and discarded, and of all known Ohio flints. Only rarely is a Lunate-edge made from a broken artifact.

Ref. 5: p 98.

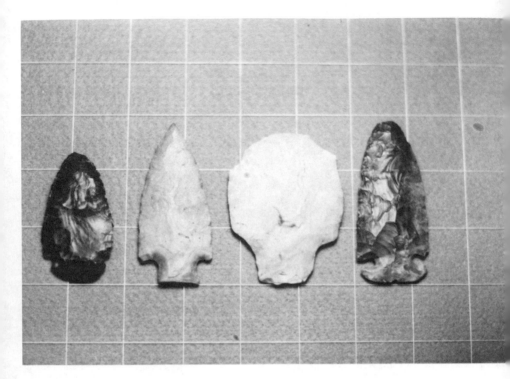

All pieces left to right:
1. Side-notched, Upper Mercer dark blue, Licking County.
2. Stemmed, Delaware County flint, Delaware County.
3. Stemmed, tan and cream flint, Licking County.
4. Enlarged-notch, brown-blue Upper Mercer, Perry County.
Hothem collection

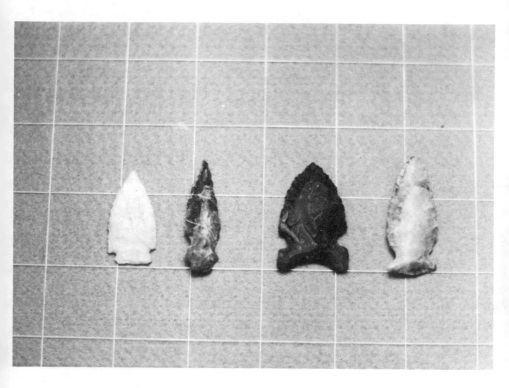

All pieces left to right:
  1. Small-notch, Flintridge jewel, Wayne County.
  2. Notched-stem, blue Upper Mercer, Delaware County.
  3. Incurvate-base, black chert, Richland County.
  4. Side-notch, unknown orange flint, Delaware County.
Hothem collection

All pieces left to right:
   1. Side-notched, grey Upper Mercer, Fairfield County.
   2. Incurvate-base, Delaware County flint, Delaware County.
   3. Serrated-edge, Indiana hornstone, Franklin County.
   4. Cylindrical, Flintridge multicolor, Fairfield County.
Hothem collection

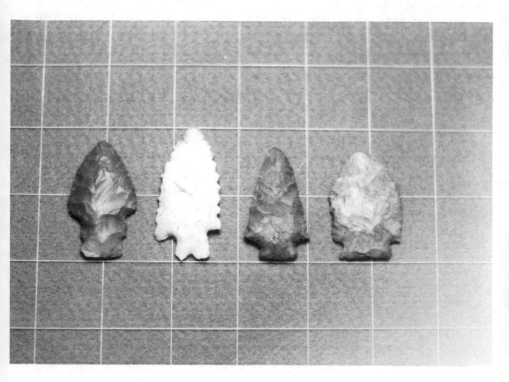

All pieces left to right:
1. Notch-stemmed, Delaware County flint, Delaware County.
2. Bifurcated, Flintridge cream, Fairfield County.
3. Notched/stemmed, unknown tan flint, Fairfield County.
4. Five-sided, mottled brown flint, Delaware County.
Hothem collection

Afterword

As research progressed for *Indian Flints of Ohio,* three patterns emerged. One is the concentration of point or knife types in the Early Archaic. (Including, no doubt, a number of the Author-named types now listed in the general Archaic category.) The number is surprisingly large, especially in view of the very limited artifact types known to be Late Paleo.

The meaning of such divergent flint artifact styles in Ohio is unclear, but certainly relates both to increased Indian population and changed lifeways - - more artifacts and more artifact styles. The large number of knife forms in the Archaic suggests that *Atl-atl* points were made of bone, wood or antler and have not survived to the present. Possibly too, Ohio's Archaic Indians were adept at securing game with snares, drives, surrounds, deadfalls and the like. Overall, the presence of so many knives suggests an abundance of acquired game, and a lifeway that was perhaps easier than previously thought.

A second observation: In terms of point/spear/knife design - - Early Paleo period to Mississippian - - designs faded and reappeared. Thus there are unhafted, stemmed, mainly notched, notched and stemmed again and triangular or basically unhafted. Sizes and weights of flint artifacts related to purpose, heavy for early spearpoints, light for late arrowheads.

Finally, regardless of the regional directional flow of "traffic," a flint-type comparison can be made. All considered, many Ohio types seem associated with the South, and lesser but about equal numbers relate to the East and West of the state. Fewer types have association with the North into Canada, no doubt because two-thirds of that Ohio border is Lake Erie, a formidable barrier in early times.

Whatever the original sources, Ohio must be considered the heartland of prehistoric Indian flints in the eastern Midwest.

References

1. Baldwin, John, "E-Notch", THE REDSKIN. Genuine Indian Relic Society,
   1978   Inc., Vol. XIII No. 1.

2. Baldwin, John, PREHISTORIC ART—DOVETAILS. Genuine Indian Relic
   1980   Society, Inc., Vol. XV No. 3 & 4.

3. Bell, Robert E., GUIDE TO THE IDENTIFICATION OF CERTAIN
   1960   AMERICAN INDIAN PROJECTILE POINTS. Special Bulletin No. 2,
                Oklahoma Anthropological Society, Oklahoma City, OK.

4. Bierer, Bert W., INDIAN ARIFACTS IN THE SOUTHEAST—A
   1977   SKETCHBOOK. Columbia, SC.

5. Brennan, Louis A., ARTIFACTS OF PREHISTORIC AMERICA. Stackpole
   1975   Books, Harrisburg, PA.

6. Broyles, Bettye J., THE ST. ALBANS SITE. Second Preliminary Report,
   1971   No. 3, West Virginia Geological and Economic Survey, Morgantown, WV.

7. Cambron, James W., A FIELD GUIDE TO SOUTHEASTERN POINT TYPES.
   19??   Alabama.

8. Carskadden, Jeff, "Hopewellian 'Birdpoints'", OHIO ARCHAEOLOGIST.
   1980   Vol. 25 No. 2.

9. Converse, Robert N., "A Basal Notched Type", OHIO ARCHAEOLOGIST.
   1979   Vol. 29 No. 2.

10. Converse, Robert N., "Archaic Broad Bladed Stemmed Points", OHIO
    1980   ARCHAEOLOGIST. Vol. 30 No. 2.

11. Converse, Robert N., OHIO FLINT TYPES. The Archaeological Society of
    1973   Ohio.

12. Dragoo, Don W., "Archaic Hunters of the Upper Ohio Valley", ANNALS OF
    1962   CARNEGIE MUSEUM. Vol. 35, Pittsburgh, PA.

13. Dragoo, Don W., MOUNDS FOR THE DEAD. (ADV reprint), Annals of
    1963   Caregie Museum, Vol. 37, Pittsburgh, PA.

14. Edler, Robert W., "A Late Archaic Point Type from Southern Indiana",
    1976   ARTIFACTS. Vol. 6 No. 3.

15. Edler, Robert W. Personal correspondence. February, 1986.
    1986

16. Fogelman, Gary L., "Bifurcated Base Points", THE PENNSYLVANIA
    1983   ARTIFACT SERIES. Booklet No. 2.

17. Fogelman, Gary L., "The Point Is...", INDIAN-ARTIFACT MAGAZINE.
    1983   Vol. 2 No. 4.

18. Funk, Robert E., "Post-Pleistocene Adaptions", HANDBOOK OF NORTH
    1978   AMERICAN INDIANS—NORTHEAST. Vol. 15, Smithsonian Institution,
                Washington, DC.

19. Glass, S.A. DVM, RETURN TO FOX FIELDS—THE MASON COUNTY,
    1984   KENTUCKY FT. ANCIENT SITE. Privately published, 2nd edition,
                Maysville, KY.

20. Goodwin, H.L., "Square-End Knives", CENTRAL STATES
    1977   ARCHAEOLOGICAL JOURNAL. Vol. 24 No. 1.

21. Gramly, Richard M., THE VAIL SITE—A PALAEO-INDIAN ENCAMPMENT
    1982   IN MAINE. Bulletin of the Buffalo Society of Natural Science, Buffalo
                NY.

22. Griffin, James B., THE FORT ANCIENT ASPECT. University
    1966   of Michigan Anthropological Papers No. 28.

23. Hart, Steven, "Black Ohio Flint Knives", ARCHAEOLOGY
    1981   '81. Genuine Indian Relic Society, Inc., Vol. XVI No. 1.

24. Harter, R.L., "Hafted Shaft Scrapers of Ohio—A
    1970   Preliminary Report", OHIO ARCHAEOLOGIST. Vol. 20 No. 1.

25. Harter, R.L., "The Early Archaic", OHIO
    1973   ARCHAEOLOGIST. Vol 23 No. 2.

26. Hastings, Jerry, "A New Bifurcated Point For Ohio", OHIO
    1971   ARCHAEOLOGIST. Vol. 21 No. 4.

27. Hastings, Jerry, "Some Kanawha Stemmed Points From
    1970   Southern Ohio", OHIO ARCHAEOLOGIST. Vol. 20 No. 3.

28. Hothem, Lar, COLLECTING INDIAN KNIVES. Books
    1986   Americana, Florence, AL.

29. Hothem, Lar, ARROWHEADS & PROJECTILE POINTS.
    1983   Collector Books, Paducah, KY.

30. Hothem, Lar, NORTH AMERICAN INDIAN ARTIFACTS. 2nd
    1982   edition, Books Americana, Florence, AL.

31. Hothem, Lar, "The Point Is...Adena—Glacial Lake", INDIAN-
    1982   ARTIFACT MAGAZINE. Vol. 1 No. 2.

32. Hothem, Lar, "The Point Is...Archaic Side-Notch--Hopewell
    82/83   Bladelets--Duo-Bevel", INDIAN-ARTIFACT MAGAZINE. Vol. 1 No. 4.

33. Hothem, Lar, "The Point Is...Fish-spear--Bottleneck",
    1982   INDIAN-ARTIFACT MAGAZINE. Vol 1 No. 3.

34. Hothem, Lar, "The Point Is...Lake Erie Bifurcates",
    1984   INDIAN-ARTIFACT MAGAZINE. Vol. 3 No. 3.

35. Hothem, Lar, "The Point Is... Paleo Knives", INDIAN-
    1985   ARTIFACT MAGAZINE. Vol. 4 No. 4.

36. Hothem, Lar, "The Point Is... Paleo Tools", INDIAN-
    1985   ARTIFACT MAGAZINE. Vol. 4 No. 2.

37. Kneberg, Madeline, "Chipped Stone Artifacts of the
    1972   Tennessee Valley Area", TEN YEARS OF THE TENNESSEE AR-
                CHAEOLOGIST. Vol. II, Tennessee Archaeological Society, Knoxville,
                TN.

38. Kneberg, Madeline, "Some Important Projectile Point
    1972   Types...", TEN YEARS OF THE TENNESSEE ARCHAEOLOGIST. Vol. II,
                Tennessee Archaeological Society, Knoxville, TN.

39. Kuhn, David W. and James W. Miller, "What Culture
    1976   Ohio 'Birdpoints'?", OHIO ARCHAEOLOGIST. Vol. 26 No. 1.

40. Lewis, Thomas and Madeline Kneberg Lewis, EVA—AN ARCHAIC
    1961   SITE. University of Tennessee Study in Anthropology, Knoxville, TN.

41. MacDonald, George F., DEBERT—A PALEO-INDIAN SITE IN CENTRAL
    1985   NOVA SCOTIA. Persimmon Press, Buffalo, NY.

42. Mayer-Oakes, William J., PREHISTORY OF THE UPPER
    1955   OHIO VALLEY. Annals of Carnegie Museum, Vol. 34, Pittsburgh, PA.

43. Mills, Truman B., "The Ulrich Group of Mounds", OHIO
    1919   ARCHAEOLOGICAL AND HISTORICAL SOCIETY PUBLICATIONS. Vol.
              XXVIII, Columbus, OH.

44. Mills, William C., "Escavations of the Adena Mound",
    1902   OHIO ARCHAEOLOGICAL AND HISTORICAL SOCIETY PUBLICATIONS.
              Vol. X, Columbus, OH.

45. Mills, William C., "The Feurt Mounds and Village Site",
    1918   OHIO ARCHAEOLOGICAL SOCIETY PUBLICATIONS. Vol XXVI, Colum-
              bus, OH.

46. Mills, William C., "Flint Ridge", OHIO ARCHAEOLOGICAL AND
    1921   HISTORICAL SOCIETY PUBLICATIONS. Vol. XXX, Columbus, OH.

47. Moffett, Ross, "The Raisch-Smith Site", OHIO STATE
    1949   ARCHAEOLOGICAL AND HISTORICAL QUARTERLY. Vol. 58, Colum-
              bus, OH.

48. Moorehead, Warren K., PREHISTORIC IMPLEMENTS. Drake reprint, Union
    1972   City, GA.

49. Mortine, Wayne A., "The Keiser Site: A Palaeo-Indian Site in Tuscarawas
    1968   County", OHIO ARCHAEOLOGIST. Vol. 18 No. 1.

50. Morton, James and Jeff Carskadden, "Excavation of an Archaic Open
    1975   Site", OHIO ARCHAEOLOGIST. Vol 25 No. 2.

51. Murphy, James L., AN ARCHEOLOGICAL HISTORY OF THE HOCKING VALLEY.
    1975   Ohio University Press, Athens, OH.

52. OHIO ARCHAEOLOGIST. Photo p. 22, 3rd row 3rd piece from right, Vol. 26 No.4.
    1976

53. Oplinger, Jon, WISE ROCKSHELTER. Kent State Research Papers in Archaeology
    1981   No. 2, KSUP, Kent, OH.

54. Painter, Floyd, "Lancets--Unusual Items From Paleo Man's Tool Kit", THE
    1985   WILLIAMSON SITE. Ed. by Rodney Peck, Harrisburg, NC.

55. Painter, Floyd, "Paleo Man's Tool Kit", THE WILLIAMSON Site. Ed. by Rodney
    1985   Peck, Harrisburg, NC.

56. Peck, Rodney M, INDIAN PROJECTILE POINT TYPES FROM VIRGINIA AND THE
    1982   CAROLINAS. Privately printed, Harrisburg, NC.

57. Perino, Gregory, GUIDE TO THE IDENTIFICATION OF CERTAIN AMERICAN INDIAN
    1974   PROJECTILE POINTS. Special Bulletin No. 3, Oklahoma Anthropological
              Society, Oklahoma City, OK.

58. Perino, Gregory, SELECTED PREFORMS, POINTS AND KNIVES OF THE NORTH
    1985   AMERICAN INDIANS. Vol. I, Idabel, OK.

59. Perino, Gregory, "Some Illinois Hopewell Cores", ARTIFACTS. Vol. 5 No. 1.
    1975

60. Pickenpaugh, Thomas E., "Projectile Points From the Brokaw Site", OHIO
    1980   ARCHAEOLOGIST. Vol. 30 No. 1.

61. Pi-Sunyer, Oriol, et al., "The Honey Run Site", STUDIES IN OHIO
    1967   ARCHAEOLOGY. Western Reserve University Press, Cleveland, OH.

62. Pliszka, Stan, "Black River Site: A Late Palaeo-Indian Camp", OHIO
    1978   ARCHAEOLOGIST. Vol. 28 No. 2.

63. Potter, Martha A., OHIO'S PREHISTORIC PEOPLES. The Ohio Historical Society,
    1968   Columbus, OH.

64. Prufer, Olaf H., "Chesser Cave", STUDIES IN OHIO ARCHAEOLOGY. Western
    1967   Reserve University Press, Cleveland, OH.

65. Prufer, Olaf H. and Raymond S. Baby, PALAEO—INDIANS OF OHIO. The Ohio
    1963   Historical Society, Columbus, OH.

66. Prufer, Olaf H., RAVEN ROCKS. Kent State Research Papers in Archaeology
    1981   No. 1, KSU Press, Kent, OH.

67. Quimby, George I., INDIAN LIFE IN THE UPPER GREAT LAKES. The University
    1960   of Chicago Press, Chicago, IL.

68. Reardon, Maurice S., "Archaic Hafted Shaft Scrapers", OHIO ARCHAEOLOGIST.
    1969   Vol. 19 No. 4.

69. Ritchie, William A., TYPOLOGY AND NOMENCLATURE OF NEW YORK
    1971   PROJECTILE POINTS. Bulletin No. 384, Revised, Albany, NY.

70. Steele, William A., "Variety In Southern Illinois Hafted Scrapers", CENTRAL
    1986   STATES ARCHAEOLOGICAL JOURNAL. Vol. 33 No. 1.

71. Tomak, Curtis H., "A Note On The Distribution of Riverton Points", CENTRAL
    1982   STATES ARCHAEOLOGICAL JOURNAL. Vol. 29 No. 1.

72. Tuck, James A., "Regional Cultural Development", HANDBOOK OF NORTH
    1978   AMERICAN INDIANS—NORTHEAST. Vol. 15, Smithsonian Institution,
              Washington, DC.

73. Tully, Lawrence N., FLINT BLADES AND PROJECTILE POINTS OF THE NORTH
    1986   AMERICAN INDIANS. Collector Books, Paducah, KY.

74. Tully, Lawrence N., Personal correspondence, March, 1986.
    1986

75. Waldorf, D.C. and Valerie Waldorf, FLINT TYPES OF THE CONTINENTAL
    1976   UNITED STATES. Privately published.

76. Webb, William S., INDIAN KNOLL. The University of Tennessee Press,
    1974   Knoxville, TN.

77. Webb, William S. and Charles E. Snow, THE ADENA PEOPLE. The University
    1974   of Tennessee Press, Knoxville, TN.

78. Winsch, John MD, "Bottlenecks or Table Rock Points", No. 9 of Series,
    1976   ARTIFACTS. Vol. 6 No. 2.

79. Winsch, John MD, "The 'Fishspear' Point", No. 11 of Series, ARTIFACTS.
    1977   Vol. 7 No. 1.

80. Winsch, John MD, "The Fractured Base or Decatur Point", No. 4 of Series,
    1975   ARTIFACTS. Vol. 5 No. 1.

81. Winsch, John MD, "Jack's Reef Corner-Notched and Raccoon Notched Points",
    1975   No. 5 of Series, ARTIFACTS. Vol. 5 No. 2.

82. Winsch, John MD, "LeCroy or Lake Erie Bifurcated Points", No. 6 of Series,
    1975   ARTIFACTS. Vol. 5 No. 3.

83. Winsch, John MD, "Pentagonal Points", No. 7 of Series, ARTIFACTS.
    1975   Vol. 5 No. 4.

84. Wormington, H.M., ANCIENT MAN IN NORTH AMERICA. Denver Museum of
    1957   Natural History Popular Series No. 4, Denver, CO.

85. Wormington H.M. and Richard G. Forbis, AN INTRODUCTION TO THE
    1965   ARCHAEOLOGY OF ALBERTA, CANADA. Denver Museum of Natural
              History, No. 11, Denver, CO.

185